Courageous
Butterfly

To Natalie,

Be yourself, you are
beautiful

Love Nancy

August 30, 2011

Courageous Butterfly

A journey to self-acceptance –
A message of hope, love and courage.

Nancy Forbes

BALBOA
PRESS
A DIVISION OF HAY HOUSE

Copyright © 2011 Nancy Forbes

All rights reserved. No part of this book may be used or reproduced by any means, graphic, electronic, or mechanical, including photocopying, recording, taping or by any information storage retrieval system without the written permission of the publisher except in the case of brief quotations embodied in critical articles and reviews.

Balboa Press books may be ordered through booksellers or by contacting:

Balboa Press
A Division of Hay House
1663 Liberty Drive
Bloomington, IN 47403
www.balboapress.com
1-(877) 407-4847

Because of the dynamic nature of the Internet, any web addresses or links contained in this book may have changed since publication and may no longer be valid. The views expressed in this work are solely those of the author and do not necessarily reflect the views of the publisher, and the publisher hereby disclaims any responsibility for them.

The author of this book does not dispense medical advice or prescribe the use of any technique as a form of treatment for physical, emotional, or medical problems without the advice of a physician, either directly or indirectly. The intent of the author is only to offer information of a general nature to help you in your quest for emotional and spiritual well-being. In the event you use any of the information in this book for yourself, which is your constitutional right, the author and the publisher assume no responsibility for your actions.

Any people depicted in stock imagery provided by Thinkstock are models,
and such images are being used for illustrative purposes only.
Certain stock imagery © Thinkstock.

ISBN: 978-1-4525-3321-6 (sc)
ISBN: 978-1-4525-3323-0 (hc)
ISBN: 978-1-4525-3322-3 (e)

Library of Congress Control Number: 2011926103

Printed in the United States of America

Balboa Press rev. date: 4/20/2011

This book is dedicated

To my husband, the love of my life, my grounding force.
To my children, the greatest accomplishment of my life.
To Jessy, the angel in my life.
And to everyone who needs hope, love, and courage.

Nancy Forbes

*No matter how long your journey appears to be,
there is never more than this:
one step, one breath, one moment—now.*

—Eckhart Tolle

CONTENTS

Foreword xi
Acknowledgments xiii
Introduction xvii
Chapter 1. My Early Years 1
Chapter 2. Teenage Years 9
Chapter 3. The Wild Escape 19
Chapter 4. Sweet Jessy 31
Chapter 5. The Incessant Dialogue 53
Chapter 6. The Winding Road to Recovery 65
Chapter 7. Yoga 93
Chapter 8. Yesterday, a wise young man spoke 109
Chapter 9. The Whispers 117
Chapter 10. The Ego Speaks Hard 135

Short Stories

Personal Messages 151
The Monkey Mind 155
The Truth 159
Closeness with God 165
God Is Love, Love Is God 169
The Greatest Gifts 173
A Precious Moment 177
Coming Back to Love 183
Fly Away 191
The Art of Moderation 195

The Power of Friendship 199
Whispering, "I love you." 203
It's Okay to Ask for What
    We Want 207
I Will Live this Day,
    and Love this Day 213
The Power of Letting Go 217
People Pleaser 221
A Knock from Heaven 225
How Can We Help? 231

Self-Healing Mantra 235
Afterword 239

FOREWORD

I am honored to have been asked to write these few words about my relationship with Nancy Forbes.

I first met Nancy when she joined one of my yoga classes. This lovely young woman would arrive in class every week, and every week I would wonder why she was here. She could not settle with the poses, gazed out the window, could not connect with her breath or relax at all. She was not comfortable with my touch and seemed to want to rush through the class to leave as quickly as possible. I was so sure that she was a student who would simply drop out.

However, Nancy came to class every single week. Week after week, she would arrive and begin her practice. Nancy did not find the poses difficult. What seemed to be difficult was understanding that yoga was not just about this pose or that pose. Slowly ... oh, so slowly, over a few years, her yoga began to change. She began to understand the asanas (poses) and pranayama (breathing). She started to focus inward, and finally let her shoulders come to rest.

As yoga teachers, we have no idea of the emotional and physiological makeup of students who come to work with us unless they tell us. A new student has not yet learned to trust the teacher and so, often, nothing is said. It is our job as yoga teachers to begin with no judgment and no expectations. We allow whatever time is required for students to begin to let down their walls when they are ready to do so.

And that is what happened with Nancy. Eventually, she shared her story with me and I am grateful for that trust.

Nancy went on to join my two-year teacher-training course and is now a full-time yoga teacher, teaching in English and in French. Her personal yoga practice has completely changed and will continue to evolve and deepen. She arrives in class with shining eyes, a big smile, and a confident walk. She brings her invaluable life experiences to her work and understands on a deep level the need to allow each student to walk his or her own path under her guidance.

This way of teaching is a gift, and Nancy's students receive that gift every time they come to her class.

—Helen Duquette

ACKNOWLEDGMENTS

I would like to thank my parents, my sisters, and my sweet son Jessy. The pain I have suffered through all of those years has given me the strength to stand tall today, and to tell my story, which is a celebration of my healing. I am through with crying, and I wish to tell my story to liberate myself. Writing my story will not only help me but others as well. In the journey through life, we all experience difficult times; my story is full of tears, tears of despair, tears of anger, but also tears of joy. This book is not only my story; it may be yours as well. I have my suffering to thank, and the depression and panic, which were sent to save me from the exaggerated behaviour I was prone to over many years. My soul was using the intolerance and hypersensitivity to warn me something was seriously wrong. In fact, they did me a great service; they led me to a better understanding of myself.

I also want to thank my husband for being my best friend for the past twenty-four years, and for believing in me, for loving me, and most of all, for never losing faith in me. Thank you for putting up with me day after day, night after night, while I was writing, reading, searching, writing, reading, searching …

Thank you, my children, for your patience and love; you are the greatest accomplishment of my life, and always will be.

To my son Spencer, thank you for letting me use your computer for four years, which allowed me to write this book. You were very tolerant. I cannot remember how many times you wanted to kick me out of your chair so as you could play with your computer games or chat with friends on Facebook, but you never did. Thanks for keeping me company on all the long walks we took together; I do appreciate it.

To my son Tyeson, thank you for all the many times we talked; those great conversations gave me the inspiration and courage to write this book. Thank you also for allowing me to write about you. You and your brother brighten my days, always.

Thank you, Wendy Alexandre, for being my friend and English teacher, and for taking over my yoga class when suddenly I became ill one day. You are special and dear to me. I would also like to thank you for all the Tuesdays you spent with me working together on my book. You gave me so much of yourself; God certainly blessed me when you came into my life.

To my best friend, Sasha Hynds, you have been my friend right from the start, offering me your support and unconditional love. What would I do without you? I am so grateful for your spiritual guidance and your trust in God. You inspired me to write my story from my heart, and all through the twenty-five years we've known each other, you have cared about who I am, where I am going, and what I am doing—you are truly a good friend. You have helped me to spread my wings and to succeed in my life. I've emerged from a dark cocoon into a radiant butterfly with your support, love, and faith. From my heart to yours, thank you for being here with me.

I want to thank my mother-in-law, Rosemary, for taking the job of correcting my English. I also want to thank her for all of her help. I've truly grown to accept, appreciate, and love her.

This book could not have been written without listening to God's whispers. It has been a learning, educational, and comforting time for me. Thank you, God, for all the inspiration you have sent me, for the love, the wisdom, and for showing me the way home. I've finally found myself and opened my heart. Thank you for making a path for me, allowing me to use my wings and visions, and making it possible for me to soar and spread a message of love throughout the world.

WALKING MY WAY HOME

Walking along a path of pain,
provoking waves of growth,
marching alone, I heard whispers,
and to my heart He spoke.

One foot rise, and one foot fall,
my dormant self aroused.
I found God surrounds us,
I saw sunshine through the clouds.

Marching gracefully along,
marching gratefully each day,
I am walking happily,
along life's stony way.

Although sometimes I stumble,
perhaps could even fall,
I know that God is watching.
He's with us one and all.

Cheerfully walking my way home
with God now every day,
brave of heart I'm walking
along my chosen way.

—Nancy Forbes
October 22, 2007

INTRODUCTION

My desire to help and connect with others is greater than any fear.
I continually struggled with the decision about whether I was capable or talented enough to write a book. Was I creative and resourceful enough to do so? Being a school dropout, and French Canadian as well, I lacked the necessary English writing skills. As a result, I doubted my ability to write my story. My fears were always my biggest enemy—the fear of what people would think of me, the fear of not being good enough, the fear of being exposed, the fear of lacking the inspiration I needed, and also the fear of offending people, and of course, the fear of failure. In the past, when the idea of putting a book came to me, I would get excited, I would be inspired for days, and yet doubt would still come to sabotage my dream. My cynical way of thinking was constantly a downer.

How good do you think you are? Who would want to read your story? I kept thinking to myself.

Terrified of the uncertainty, I procrastinated, yet never stopped dreaming. I have kept a journal since I was fifteen years old. In November 2004, at the age of forty, I stopped writing, and for two years, I abandoned recording my life on paper. It seemed that the passion had gone—until the magical night of February 9, 2007. I shall take you through this chapter of my life, but before going there, I would like to share with you the foundation, the footprint of my story, the beginning. To understand my path—the road to self-acceptance—you need to know where I was mentally and emotionally in my early years, and who I became because of it, and later, you will see who I am today. I can finally say I love who I am, because I am finally giving myself permission to be me.

As you read the first chapters of my life story, please keep in mind that I now call my past *so what*. I am not bitter, I am not resentful, I am not a victim. I am no longer in that place, although I do not like to talk about the past, since I now understand the effect my thoughts and words have on my well-being. However, to write this book, I am willing to go there once again.

My past is simply a story—*my* story. The reason for writing about it is to offer you three wonderful expressions of life, *Hope*, *Love*, and *Courage*; to reveal that in time, we have to move on, to awaken, to evolve, to grow up, but most importantly, we have to remember where we came from—*who we really are*. We must stop blaming and feeling sorry for ourselves. We have to be responsible for our own lives, and if we have to, we must create ourselves anew.

Even though today I call my past *so what*, during the writing of this book, I revived a lot of old pain, experiencing first hand the power of my thoughts. While writing, I had allowed my past to resurface and let my mind experience the drama all over again; as a result of this, the emotional pain of my upbringing materialized, making it impossible for me to feel good while writing my story. Fortunately, this time, I was aware of what I was doing. I understood why I felt this way. I could shift my attention to the present moment at any time and instantly make a difference in how I was feeling. This is how powerful our thoughts truly are!

Although I am considering my past as stepping-stones, gifts that served me well, I learned that the past can also trap us in vicious cycles of pain, and fear can immobilize and stop us from moving forward.

True power is when we are fully present and recognizing that reality exists only in the *now*. Freedom will come in the awareness of loving and trusting life, moment by moment, day after day.

Trust in that.

TO MY READERS,

I'm taking you through the events of my early life only to enable you to understand how I arrived where I am today. I do not wish to dwell on the past, as this is a book of inspiration, love and hope. This is my true intended message. Owning my story, revealing my deepest secrets, embracing my fears and loving myself in the process has been the bravest and the most freeing experience of my life. We all have secrets, and by sharing them, we take away the power they have over us, and gives us a chance to connect with others. I understand the risk in putting my truth out in the world. However, there is an even bigger risk in hiding it.

    I believed it all started with my given name. For thirty-five years, my name, Nancy Forbes, did not feel right to me. As a result, I felt extremely uncomfortable in my body. When someone would ask me my name, it triggered an awful feeling, a sense of not belonging and not knowing where I came from. It truly troubled my heart. I would think to myself, *Why is it so hard for me to hear or say my own name? Why do I not recognize this name as mine?*

    Who am I? I asked myself.

    Was I born to the right family? Am I the only one in this world who feels this way, disconnected from their given names? As weird as this may sound, I felt like an outsider, an absolute stranger to myself. I never mentioned this to anyone—it felt too weird and embarrassing. I felt lonely with this painful secret for so long, until now.

Who is this person with the name Nancy Forbes?

As a young child, I believed my name interfered with my happiness. I remember constantly struggling with extreme loneliness and feeling as if I did not belong anywhere or with anyone. I would constantly and frantically think to myself, *Why do I feel so out of touch, so alone, so different?* I lived with this awful feeling most of my life. I wished and dreamed for a new name, hoping to feel better about myself.

At the time, I assumed my name represented who I was, the real me. I was trying to find myself by demanding to *feel* my name so I could finally find my own identity.

Am I a lost soul? I wondered.

I was confused. I never thought that I was more than just a name, a name that felt foreign to me, and so much so that I continuously asked myself whether or not to change it.

Who am I? I asked myself again and again.

Most of my life I struggled and suffered. It has taken me years to remember who I really am and to create myself anew. I am always discovering, learning, and working towards my personal growth, and today, I can finally say that I am comfortable with the sound of my name, Nancy Forbes.

I chose to remember where I came from. As a result, I discovered life, God, and therefore my Self. My soul represents who I am, not my name. My true essence is my heart—it is the *love* behind the neurotic mind. I truly exist within the awareness.

I have learned to accept *what is*—the things that I cannot change, and finding the courage to change the things I can. This was the starting point of my transformation into a beautiful butterfly. In the midst of learning how to fly, I've liberated myself in order to reveal my true spirit.

I like to contemplate and write about life. When I write, time no longer exists for me, and I feel inspired, never alone. When I pick up a pen, I look for space in my mind, inviting my spirit to join in. I am always looking for insight and wisdom. My years of yoga became part of my *soul* searching. After years of questioning who I am, I discovered the true purpose of my life, which is sharing the power of *love* with those around me. I have experienced a number of incredible things, which I would like to share with you. My findings are in relationship to my ordinary daily life, the step-by-step lessons of my experiences, and the *gifts* that came with them. I have written about real events, true feelings, and life lessons that I have learned and gathered over the years.

On February 9, 2007, I was sitting in bed pondering, and I thought that my life has been like a soap opera; I have faced so many challenges and have so many interesting and entertaining stories to share. My healing empowered me to speak the truth, and I have a powerful message to tell. I want to open a world of great possibility and hope. By sharing both the joy and pain of my own transformation, and by telling the truth about my vulnerabilities, I hope to offer encouragement and to inspire anyone who needs help and desires to create themselves anew.

I am ready to break out of my comfort zone, my cocoon, to fly on this journey with you—believe me, we are never alone in this world.

Hope, Love, and Courage, from my heart to yours,

Nancy Forbes

Chapter One
MY EARLY YEARS

I was only five years old when my sisters Sylvie, six and a half, Johanne, three, and I were placed in a convent outside Montréal. I remember that terrifying period of my life, recalling how frightened and shocked I was when our parents abandoned us. Terrified of the unknown, we were left with strangers without any explanation of why or when our parents would come back for us. A war started to rage inside me, fear took over my tiny body, and I could not understand why my mother had left us. Minutes turned into hours, then hours turned into days, and the weight of the rejection began to rip my heart apart. Overwhelmed by fright, I curled up into a ball and cried for days. I hurt from the very core of my being; that was the beginning of my intense suffering.

With a broken heart, fear seemed to be the only emotion left in me. At this very young age, I had set in motion soul-pain feeling unwanted, unloved, unworthy, and unaware that this baggage would follow me for most of my life. Yet during those terrible months, I had also set in motion my survival instincts. Somehow, I found the strength to survive every obstacle that came my way. I stood for long hours inside a crib, in wet diapers the nuns had forced on me. Humiliated, I waited and waited. I waited for the return of my mother.

As time passed, exhaustion took over, and this allowed me to sleep. It was a brief release from my deep sadness, but only until my eyes opened again. After weeks of endless tears, I finally stopped waiting. I felt trapped; morning to night, I lay in the crib and used my imagination to pass the excruciating hours of seclusion. Behind bars in a crib, like a bird in a cage, I felt abandoned and neglected by everyone, including my parents. The three long months felt like an eternity. I was only five years old, and I lived through my first experience of isolation and abandonment.

The bittersweet return

Home again, my parents tried to reconcile their differences for almost two years. This interlude resulted in two more children, twin girls, Chantal and Sonia. We were now five innocent little girls, ranging from the age of one and a half to eight, in a very dysfunctional household. My father was constantly missing and seldom supported his family. My mother was struggling for money and time, and she worked long hours in a distressed state of mind. Running out of patience, she became overwhelmed with responsibilities and decided to leave our father and send us away. Déjà-vue! As I recalled the pain of our previous separation, I became hysterical and out of control. I cried and begged my mother not to leave me again. I was overwhelmed with fear, as I knew what to expect—the abandonment, the loneliness, and the excruciatingly long wait. I remember crying out, "How long, Mom? How long this time, Mom?"

The very first night at the convent of Centre Térèse-Martin, I cried so hard that I threw up all over my bed and on the stuffed animal that my mother had given me for Christmas, my own precious lion. My insides were torn to shreds; my lion was the only friend I had in the whole world, and I had vomited all over him. That little ball of fur was my only comfort, my companion. It was the most precious possession I owned. I felt my mother's gentle touch in the comfort of its soft, warm fur. I was devastated. I could no longer press my little furry friend against my chest to feel my mother's love. Scared of the reaction of the nuns, I got up, removed my sheets, took them along with my lion to the washroom, and tried desperately to wash them clean. I then returned to bed, carrying with me a very wet stuffed animal. I rested my head on the pillow, squeezing my only friend in the world close to my heart, and waiting forever to fall asleep in a cold, naked bed.

My sisters and I were making a great effort to survive and trying to understand the new situation. We had been separated from each other. Sylvie and I stayed at the convent Centre Térèse-Martin and my younger sisters were put in foster homes. I was only seven years old, facing my second horrific "left behind" abandonment. Little did we know that this time, the wait would be *five* long years! Even though Sylvie and I were living in the same center, we were separated from the start. We had been placed in two different dormitories, walls and floors apart, so we could only see each other at meal times. My eyes would hunt through the large, noisy cafeteria, hoping to have a glimpse of my sister, desperately looking for a familiar face. My life was upside down; nothing made sense any more. I was sitting only a few feet away from my older sister and yet I was unable to reach her. I wanted to scream, "Let me go, let me be with my sister. I need my life to make sense again." But I was trapped. Someone else was in charge of my every move. I couldn't do what I knew in my heart was right. I had to walk their way, speak their way, and follow their rules. At all times, I had to be obedient and well mannered to meet their expectations. I was forbidden to sit with or talk to my older sister.

To survive Centre Térèse-Martin we had to be good little girls, and luckily, somehow, I managed to do that. I was leaning to survive.

The following year my sister Johanne came to stay with us. I remember clearly the terrifying moment when I was forced to ignore

3

her. I could not protect, comfort or hold her. Johanne was now living with her two older sisters, Sylvie and me, yet walls and floors still kept us apart. On her first day in the cafeteria, Johanne's big brown eyes looked lost and sad. While standing in line with her classmates, she stared in frozen silence at the sitting area. My heart pounded. I was in so much pain to see her so frightened. Her eyes began wandering across the room until she noticed me. Only ten feet away from her, I was anxiously waiting for her eyes to reach mine. When finally they found me, she smiled.

Johanne was only five and a half years old and to me, she looked undersized, too fragile to be here with us, and yet, she kept smiling. I had a deep and profound desire to hold her in my arms, to let her know that I was there for her, but it was forbidden. Johanne was surrounded by many lost little souls just like mine. I stared at her big brown eyes and cried inside, *Don't be frightened Johanne, I am here for you. Except, I can't reach you. I'm sorry. I am so sorry.*

I felt powerless to help her.

Today's reflection: My sister Johanne

So many years have passed since I last saw my sister Johanne. I can't believe that the last time we spoke was ten years ago. I still want to hold and protect her, although this time, I know it's really up to her.

For over twenty-five years now, Johanne has chosen to follow a strict religious organization with very strong convictions. For her it's the only way to God's ultimate love. I have chosen a different path to meet God—not that my way is a better way, but Johanne has decided to break all ties with our family. We tried for years to reach her, but failed every time. I have decided to let her go and to let God protect her. I love my sister and I respect her decision, and by surrendering and accepting *what is*, I know I have freed her and myself from more suffering.

However, I am letting her go with an open heart. Whenever she is ready, I will be right here to meet her with open arms.

I love you, Johanne
I miss you so very much

1971: The excruciatingly long wait, at the age of eight

Sylvie, Johanne, and I were able to visit my mother almost every other weekend, and for that short time, my mother's kind words of love would help us to survive the wait. She would say, "Soon, very soon, we will be together again." However, time would pass and her words left me drowning in disappointment and in a deep silent sadness. Every day I dreamed of our reunion, but week after week, there was nothing but heartbreak and disappointment, just another month of grief—another year of disillusionment. For five anxious little girls, the word "soon" meant days, possibly months, but certainly not five years. I was losing hope, I was losing faith. Every single night, I prayed to God, "Please reunite my family, and I promise that I will be a very good little girl." Nevertheless, five long years passed, and it seemed to me that I spent my whole childhood in a convent. I was twelve years old before my family was reunited. Finally, I was living with my mother and sisters, and nothing else mattered. I don't even recall feeling angry about what had happened. I was too high with relief to be resentful. For a while, I lived in the moment, enjoying every minute of my freedom. It seemed that I had let go of the past and was moving quickly forward. Adjusting to my new surroundings came easily. We had a wonderful new house, I had a bedroom I loved, and I adored my new school. However, adjusting to my mother's boyfriend, who became my "sort-of stepfather," was another story. It did not take too long for us to dislike his ways of parenting. He was short-tempered, cold and demanding, constantly screaming to intimidate us. He had no trouble demonstrating that he did not want us there. I was scared of him from the beginning. However, Lucien was the reason we were all together as a family, so we had to endure his presence and his rules.

It became more and more difficult to live with him. We had to ask his permission for everything: to go out with friends, to watch television, to listen to music, to take a bath, to eat, and even to speak. He had no tolerance. Our cheerfulness annoyed him, so he stopped us from playing and being childlike. He ruined our newfound happiness. It didn't matter what day or time it was, when he was around, we had to be extremely quiet and well behaved. It was very stressful for five little girls who desperately needed to experience love and playtime, and to have a little freedom. Forbidden to be a child, my life became a prison once again. The dreadful feeling of not belonging soon came back to haunt me.

"God, where do I belong?" I questioned again.

The obsession with questioning my identity started around that time. By the age of twelve my given name meant nothing to me; in fact, it troubled me. A few months following our family's reunion, my hopes and dreams were shattered. With little concern for our happiness, my sisters and I were forced to survive in a house full of tension and extreme demands. When things got too out of hand, my mother would try to ease the pain. She would share a smile and giggle with us without my stepfather knowing. It was her gentle way of telling us to listen and do whatever he said in order to keep the peace.

At times, when everyone else was asleep, my mother would come into my bedroom. She would gently wake me up so as we could talk. At such times, I realized how much she truly loved us. My mother knew how difficult it was for us, but felt she couldn't do anything about it, as Lucien was the reason we were all together.

I saw my mother cry frequently, and I knew her heart was breaking. She wanted security and a refuge for her children. She endured and suffered as much as we did. When Lucien would leave for work, the tension and negative energy left with him. Then, and only then, would we be able to breathe and laugh again together with my mother.

For six long years, I tried to cope while I waited, waited to grow up so I could move out and maybe fall in love. I wanted to have someone to be with, and wanted to belong somewhere.

Caught in a haze, I often saw myself standing in the middle of the world—alone.

"Is there a place for me here?" I wondered.

Chapter Two
TEENAGE YEARS

Although it was wrong from the start, I fell in love at the age of fifteen with a sixteen-year-old boy, whom I shall refer to as Derek. Derek was a popular teenager; however he was always getting in trouble. The boys respected him because they thought he was the coolest kid in town, and the girls loved him because of his attractive bad-boy image. He was six foot tall with a great smile, piercing green eyes, and long beautiful hair; he captured my heart. Unfortunately, Derek came from a very dysfunctional family, as I did. He was emotionally wounded from lack of love, attention, and parenting. He was suffering, and through his constant emotional outbursts, I suffered as well. He was subject to explosions of jealousy and was very controlling. He ordered me around constantly and criticized my every move—the way I dressed, the way I spoke, even the way I walked—not much of a change from my prior and actual life. Wanting desperately for the relationship to work, I agreed to his demands. I dressed, talked, and walked to please him. I believed this would keep the peace between us. He would then love me and then I would be happy. Being submissive had worked with the nuns and now at home. Therefore, I assumed that by following the same pattern with my boyfriend, everything would be okay. I would have someone to love me and would no longer feel alone. I jumped head first into the relationship, unaware that things were about to get worse, and I mean a lot worse. During his insecurities and fits of rage, I became his punching bag. This irrational behavior came to be a consistent affair. Wanting desperately to belong, I allowed this abuse to happen. I let him mistreat me for the three years we were together. The verbal abuse began almost immediately, and the physical abuse started shortly afterwards. At first, he pushed and called me names, and soon, I was being dragged, punched, and beaten into the ground. In the beginning, he apologized and begged for forgiveness, and I felt sorry for him, so I accepted his apologies. I allowed this to happen over and over again. I somehow believed he had the right to treat me this way.

Derek blamed me, one way or another, for his heated outbreaks. They became my fault, of course. "You are too beautiful, too nice, too friendly. Look at the way you dress. Look at the way you approach people, your walk stirred up attention, your smile is provocative. I love you so much that it makes me crazy when I see you talk to other people. It drives me insane when guys are looking at you."

I began to think that he might be right, perhaps I was too friendly, too nice, to pleasing, etc. I wanted so desperately to find someone and leave my miserable life that I changed to please him. I transformed myself to whomever he wanted me to be. I tried to look distant and less attractive, and very soon I became introverted. However, it did not matter how much I distanced myself from the world, it was never good enough for him. It did not work. He always found a reason to mistreat me, and because of my insecurities and hunger to feel loved, I slowly began to fade away. Sadly I continued to accept and tolerate his physical and mental abuse, losing myself piece by piece along the way, until one day I had all but disappeared. I had no self-esteem, no self-respect, and no self-worth left in me. I had faded into Derek's shadow. No one knew about the abuse, not even my mother. However, I know she saw bruises on my body from where I had been pushed, cut, and punched so many times, even though I was trying very hard to cover them and find excuses for each mark. I told my family and friends that I had fallen off my bike, hit the corner of a table, or fallen down the stairs. I even said that I had fistfights with friends. I learned how to cover up the bruises and the pain, lying to keep people from knowing my secret, the secret I was so ashamed of. I knew it was wrong and I knew one day it could kill me, but I was blinded by desperation.

It takes awareness, courage, and honesty to look at ourselves and realize our own dysfunctional behavior; if we don't face our fears, they will remain with us.

I was unaware of the heavy emotional burden I was carrying within me. I wanted to escape from my stepfather's house, and by moving in with Derek, I hoped I would be free. I thought Derek would realize he could trust me, and then he would alter his violent ways. I moved in with Derek just days before my eighteenth birthday.

How naïve I was! Moving in with Derek was the worst move of my life. He turned out to be a paranoid psycho freak. He became even more obsessive and violent. He forbade me to speak to anyone; he ripped the phone off the wall and ordered me to stay in the apartment at all times. One night, he locked me in, took the keys, and away he went. I was scared out of my mind. I was caged again; I was a prisoner, his prisoner.

Left alone like this every night, I decided to go out for a short run around the block. I had not locked the front door since I had no key. I was only gone for forty-five minutes. When I came back to the apartment, I opened the door and looked into the living room. My heart stopped! Derek was sitting on the couch with the scariest look on his face. I panicked. He jumped off the couch and swung at me. Without a sound and without putting up a fight, I let him hit me. He threw me on the floor, kicked me in the stomach, kicked my back, then my legs. He tried to punch me in the face, but I covered it with my hands. During the attack, he called me names and accused me of all kinds of nonsense. Without trying to convince him to stop, I let him do this to me, over and over again, until suddenly, the room went quiet and the abuse stopped. I stayed on the floor and tried to hide my face, not looking at him because I did not want to provoke any more violence. I stayed still and waited for him to leave. To my surprise, I felt relief. I don't know why, but I knew it was over. I knew this would be the last time he would abuse me. Something had stirred inside me; I felt different. I saw myself moving away from him. Finally, I recognized the situation for what it was—absolutely nothing. This relationship was nothing. We had nothing. It was all a big lie. "Oh, God, never again will I let anyone put their hateful hands on me."

"NEVER AGAIN!"

Derek ran out the door and I had become strangely numb. I stopped crying and gathered my thoughts. As I grew calmer, I began to see a way out. I was finally ready to make a difference in my life. I was willing to care for myself. I'd had enough.

ENOUGH!

As I lay there on the ground, I was overwhelmed with shame.

"What have I done to myself?" I moaned. "Why did I let someone treat me this way for so long? Oh, God, I did this to myself. I allowed this to happen. I let him control my life, deciding everything for me."

I cried, "I want my life back. I want my power back."

"But how? My life is such a mess."

"I am such a mess."

Then I thought to myself, *Nancy, this is your life, your body, your face, your decision, your story—find your way out. You can do this. I know you can. I trust in you.*

The ego is our pain, but it is what we know, and we resist moving out of it. The effort it takes to grow out of painful patterns often feels more uncomfortable than remaining within them. Personal growth can be painful, because it can make us feel ashamed and humiliated to face our own darkness. But the goal of personal growth is the journey out of dark emotional patterns that cause us pain, to those that create peace.

— Marianne Williamson
A Return to Love

Today's reflection

What was so different about me that night?
Why did I see the light at that very moment?

I did not recognize it then, but I certainly do now. While looking at my journals, I realized that I had prayed for the wrong things, wished for the wrong outcome. I had asked God to change my boyfriend, to change his behaviors, to change his temper. My full attention was on him, not on me, but there was truly nothing that I could have done for him. He had to see, feel, and want it for himself in order for that transformation to take place. No prayer in the world would have made him change. That work was his, not mine. I had my own issues to overcome. As I look back in my journals, I realize that not once did I ask for something for myself. All my writings were about him. "Please God, stop him from hurting me, stop him from being jealous, make him realize how much I love him, and make him see he can trust me, blah, blah, blah."

My suffering was caused by me, my low self-esteem, my lack of understanding and my lack of awareness. My happiness depended on my choices, on my own awakening, not on his. It was not his responsibility to make me happy, but I did not know that. I was unaware of my power and role in my own happiness. I was a sleepwalker in life.

My mind had one focus—him.

I had to wake up!

Talking to God is easy; everybody can do it. The hard part is listening to the answers. They come from the heart, a deep feeling, an inner knowing, like a strong intuition. Yet, we have to be present and willing to hear the Whispers from Heaven.

On that terrible night, my prayers changed. I no longer asked God to change my boyfriend. I prayed for insight for myself—"God, I want to be happy. I want to be free; show me the way." By changing my prayers, my life story began to change its direction. And this is why: I discovered that whatever I wrote down on paper, I also visualized in my mind. When I write about pain, I see pain, I feel pain, and I experience pain. When I write about happiness, I see joy in my mind and feel happy in my heart, and it will become my life experience.

My wish list had changed, and I began to focus on *my* freedom. This changed my writing and feelings. What we think is vital, but it's not so much what we think, but how strongly we *feel*, that creates our life experiences. Until I changed how I felt, I couldn't change my situation. Feeling is the way to communicate with the Universe; it is the language that *It* understands. Searching for a way out, I saw myself being free and wrote all about it, and then I felt it. I truly felt it. I began creating a different outcome for myself, a new story, even though I was not aware of this. The light had dawned that night; I became strong and willing again. I was ready to get out, to find my freedom. I loved myself enough to say ENOUGH. I'd had enough—no more abuse. My life did not dramatically change at that time. Yet, the change of thought definitely allowed me to move forward.

The following morning, I woke up and knew in my heart that my relationship with Derek was over. However, I had to move fast. I went to school that morning and asked a friend to help me move. Once I had explained my situation, he understood right away and agreed to help me. I had already packed my belongings and had only a few more things to gather. We needed to move quickly, and we did. I left a short note on the table, and never returned.

I'd had enough!

Even though you may look around and dislike much of what you see in your personal world, feeling trapped by other people and difficult situations, you retain the power to create a totally new hologram. A new hologram implies a new self.

—Deepak Chopra
The Shadow Effect

Before I continue with my story, I want you to know it has taken me a long time to find the courage to write about my twenties. I had pushed aside that period of my life and had never talked about it, as if it did not exist. For many years I dreaded that someone would discover my secret, and then everyone would know. Today I'm still uncomfortable revealing my past, but the day has come and I am the *one* who chooses to reveal all.

A journey to self-acceptance – A message of hope, love and courage.

My kids, oh God, my children are everything to me; this revelation could hurt them. What are they going to think when they learn my deepest secret? Will the image of their mother be shattered forever? I still have some family members who do not know what I did all those years.

How can I disclose that chapter of my life gracefully?

Can I really rid myself of those doubts and reservations?

Can I be strong and courageous enough?

I don't want to ignore my children's questions any longer. I want to stop playing games. I'm tired; I want to come clean. My children already ask too many questions. "Where did you meet Daddy, Mom? Why are you the only one in your family living in Ontario? Why did you move away from home? What kind of work did you do, Mom?" So far, I've managed to avoid their questions by manipulation and by never really finishing a conversation. However, they are getting older and they will ask again. I want my children to hear it from me and not from someone else. This is a chance to share my story with them, and I know in my heart that it is the right thing to do, and now is the time.

They are ready, I am ready; I trust in that.

Our shadow keeps us from full self-expression, from speaking our truth, and from living an authentic life. It is only by embracing our duality that we free ourselves of the behaviors that can potentially bring us down. If we don't acknowledge all of who we are, we are guaranteed to be blindsided by the shadow effect.

—Debbie Ford
The Shadow Effect

Today's reflection

I know there is a greater force out there working on my behalf. So I can let go of my fears and give up on how and when the inspiration will come. I'll trust in God's perfect plan.

On this magical winter morning, the temperature is warm and caressing, though the sky is dark and it looks like rain. It's approximately 10 degrees Celsius, way above the seasonal average; it's a wonderful day, perfect for a walk. Today is my birthday. I am now forty-five, and so I want to stop for a moment and reflect on my life.

I'm healthy and strong and I feel incredibly well. I'm in a good place in my life. I have lived on this earth for forty-five years and I'm amazed at where this life has taken me. Life is not always easy, but it is certainly good. I have grown and learned so much over the past few years. I have discovered that in every painful experience, there is some good to be found, a lesson to be learned, or a gift of some sort to be discovered. Through the years I have learned to look beyond the pain, to see the truth, and to live my life with an open heart.

"God, I ask that you join me on my walk.

"I ask for your guidance … Please inspire my thoughts, and through this vision show me the way. Provide me with the wisdom to write again. I'm blocked, and I am afraid to reveal my past. I'm wondering how to bring my twenties into this story."

When walking I become grounded, my mind is entwined with the beauty of nature. The fresh air and the song of the birds, they all help to clear my mind. With each step, I grow more receptive to my surroundings, allowing the Whispers of the Universe to enter my heart. In these moments, I am truly grateful—I am ready to receive God's light.

Two days after that birthday walk, I was sick in bed with a nasty cold, and decided to read a book my mother loaned me, called *Les secrets de Norah*, or *The secrets of Norah*, by Norah Shariff.

For a moment, I wondered if I should read her story since her biography was about her nightmarish father and her horrific sufferings. I do not like reading distressing stories; they leave me feeling depressed far too long afterwards. Still, my mother told me she gained great insight from the story and that it ended well. I love happy endings, and I also needed to be inspired. It turned out to be just what the doctor ordered, a good book and bed rest. I read it from cover to cover, in two days. While I was reading that incredible story, I asked myself, *What can I learn from her experiences? She described so much pain and suffering.* I believed there must have been a reason for me to read her story—a personal message, perhaps? I put down the book to meditate and felt a wave of strength enter my body. Suddenly I thought to myself, *I am ready. I can do this.*

I realized the fear of writing about my past was gone. Suddenly, what people thought of me didn't matter anymore. I would no longer feel embarrassed. Amazingly, I felt a great appreciation for my own story. Norah Shariff's had awakened in me the strength I needed to write again. I had absorbed her courage like a sponge.

I now see my story differently. There is nothing to be ashamed of. I am who I am today because of my experiences. I don't want my secret to control my life. I want to be set free, and most of all, I want to be me. I am ready to tell the truth and, should the fear of what people would think of me resurface, I will face it. I know who I am. I am a courageous butterfly, a perfection of God's creation. I am in the process of awakening and making a difference. It is my path to follow. My children are wonderful; they love me unconditionally, and they will be proud of the great courage it has taken to write my story.

I trust in that.

Chapter Three
THE WILD ESCAPE

1982

Soon after leaving Derek, I moved in with a friend who later became my next boyfriend. I was nineteen years old, a full-time student studying to become a psychologist. I was not working and neither was my boyfriend Mike. Mike was a nice guy and loved me, but his lack of maturity and partying drove me mad. I quickly became tired of his laziness and lack of ambition.

Mike knew my previous boyfriend, and he also knew about the abuse and how much I had suffered. I was certain that he would never put a hand on me, because NEVER again would I let anyone abuse me. I had learned a valuable lesson. However, I had another problem. Mike was irresponsible. He could not hold a job longer than a few months. I could not trust him with money. He took no responsibility for his share of the household expenses, and I had to take care of all the bills myself. The money I had received from a student loan was soon gone, and we were in trouble. No, I mean *I* was in trouble. I wanted to continue with my schooling but I needed money fast. I loved my boyfriend, but he was draining me financially. At the time, leaving him did not feel like an option, for as he was not abusing me physically, in my eyes, he was good for me.

A couple of weeks before Christmas, a girlfriend of mine, Maryse, came to visit for a few days. She told me she was also struggling financially to survive. I knew she had a difficult life, as she had been on her own since the age of fifteen. Maryse told me that she knew a friend who was working in Ontario, making lots of money, and I also knew someone who was doing the same type of work in Montréal. We talked about it all night and convinced ourselves to call an agency in the morning for more information. Without telling anyone, the following week, we were gone. Scared out of our minds, we found ourselves sitting in an agency office waiting for someone to direct us toward a bus. I tried to convince myself that we were doing the right thing, and hoped that no one would recognize us. Despite the fact that we were both frightened to death, we kept quiet. The long wait made the situation unbearable; when suddenly my eyes caught sight of the mini-van that arrived for us, I began to hyperventilate. My stomach was in knots and my mind raced. I continuously went over my options, hoping to think of a way out, but I found myself lining up, ready to enter the van. I had made a pact; I had given my word, I did not want to look weak. I hoped Maryse would chicken out, but she didn't, and so we sat in the van quietly for along time. The closer we got to Toronto the more frightened and panicky we became. Reality hit us hard; we realized that we did not know what we were doing, or should be doing. I was not prepared for this kind of work. This wise move was not so wise after all. It was impulsive and probably would be dangerous. We could not speak a word of English to save our lives. We were just two inexperienced, scared teenagers looking for work in a strange city, and we had put ourselves in a high-risk situation.

Fear engulfed my every thought. We were stuck in the mini-van for nine hours with ten other girls who seemed to know exactly what they were doing. I reluctantly surrendered to the inevitable and accepted where I was heading. I listened attentively to what the others girls were saying, pretending I had done this kind of work before. I thought by watching them, I would find out what I needed to know. There it was, the only chance to learn something before being dropped off at the front doors of a strip club. The girls were sharing every detail of their experiences with each other, talking about music, sexy moves, money, clothing, clients, and about changing their names. Each one had given herself a sexy stage name. My disconnection with my own name made this moment enjoyable. I listened carefully and absorbed whatever I needed to know to make myself fit in.

The night was cold and miserable as we arrived in Niagara Falls, Ontario. The wind seemed to push me toward the front doors of the club, and like an insecure little puppy, I followed the girls into the building. I was petrified. I tried to see inside, but it was too dark. The music was deafening and my eyes needed to adjust. Suddenly, I saw lights of every color moving in every direction, allowing me a glimpse of each corner of the room. It looked like a disco nightclub, with the exception of a huge stage in the middle of the bar, approximately four feet above the ground, twenty feet long, and maybe seven to eight feet wide. What really caught my eyes was the stunning girl who was dancing on the stage. I was surprised to see how beautiful and sophisticated she looked. Her dancing was effortless and elegant; she did not look like a rough biker girl with tattoos, like I expected; she seemed nice. At the end of her show, people were screaming and applauding; she was a star. I could not believe my eyes.

The manager greeted us at the entrance and walked us to our rooms. The bedrooms were on the second floor of the club and the showers were at the end of the corridors. Each bedroom had two single beds, and I shared my room with my partner in crime, Maryse. We listened to the rules, and did not ask questions. Asking questions would mean that we did not know what we were doing, and we were not about to admit that to anyone. Then, the manager informed us we had one hour to get ready.

"You are all working tonight," he said. "We need girls downstairs ASAP."

What! Are you out of your mind? I screamed inwardly.

I panicked, repeating in my head the man's words: "You are all working tonight and have only *one* hour to get ready!"

"I'm not ready. I can't do this right now!" I told Maryse.

"We can't even speak English to find our way back home," she said.

We were cornered, and we had put ourselves in this position voluntarily—there was no escape. "Oh, God, I think we have to do this!"

I found myself staring at my suitcases, wondering what I could wear. I could hardly believe where I was, miles away from home, in an entirely new environment about to do something so really crazy. Despite the fact that I was panicking, I still made it downstairs. As I was descending the spiral staircase, I looked at each girl who passed me by, wondering if I looked anything like them. *Can they tell? Do I look like someone who is about to humiliate herself?* I thought.

I looked around the room and saw only a crazy crowd. Girls were "working the room" and the guys were screaming like maniacs. I stepped into the club, hesitant and afraid. Approaching the DJ, I gave him my new name. "I am Gézabelle," I said. To my surprise, the DJ spoke French and we connected right away. I felt comfortable enough to tell him my secret. "I need help, it's my first time. Can you please shorten the songs? And please, don't tell anyone," I said anxiously.

Of course, the DJ told the entire club. "Please, make a lot of noise for this beautiful new French girl; her name is Gézabelle and it's her *first* time," he shouted. The guys went wild, screaming with enthusiasm, hitting the tables with bottles, and some guys even walked towards the stage to bang on the floor. I looked at the DJ, not really knowing what was happening. You could see his smile for miles; he was smirking. I could have killed him!

Totally terrified, I found myself on the stage dancing and disrobing for money. My first steps were beyond my control; my feet were moving without me even thinking about it, impulsively improvising the next move. My body was trembling uncontrollably. My legs—well, they were shaking like jackhammers. My mind—what can I say! My mind had succumbed to a moment of insanity, and then became almost numb. I was doing something completely shocking and out of character. Believe it or not, I managed to get through two weeks of this shocking work experience, and still ended up with a sense of accomplishment, plus the money I really needed. Strangely enough, I felt empowered by the experience that night. I had done something I never believed I ever could, and the desire to be self-sufficient made me appreciate the work. I believed that I had found a way out of all my troubles. What's more, I grew quickly into my new name. Gézabelle gave me a new sense of identity, I felt powerful and in control, and this new sensation brought with it what I was yearning for: recognition, validation, money, independence, and a sense of freedom. Perhaps even a place where I belonged.

All my life, I'd been waiting for someone to save me. *Perhaps it is up to me to save myself from my miserable life*, I thought. Maryse left to go home, but I stayed a little longer. A week later, I went home with enough money to pay my debts. This major success made me want to go back to Ontario as often as I could, and so I decided to go back for a week each month. On one occasion, I sent the money home for rent and stayed an extra week. Then, when I finally arrived home, I found my boyfriend had spent the rent money on partying. I was furious. I had lost weeks of school, and on top of that, owed the next month's rent and still owed the last month. Two days later, I was back in Ontario, working to pay my bills. Furious over what had happened, I questioned my relationship, and realized that my boyfriend was once again the wrong one. I wanted out! I made the decision to give up my schooling, and, of course, my immature boyfriend. There were no more reasons for me to stay in town. Just like that, I packed my bags and paid a friend to drive me to Niagara Falls, where I set myself up in a hotel next to the club without telling anyone. In the beginning, I moved around, starting with Niagara Falls, then Windsor, Hamilton, London, and then Toronto. I soon became popular, as these men seemed to like me. Many times, I didn't even have to dance—sitting and smiling was enough. They liked the fact that I was trying to speak English, walking around with a tiny dictionary, doing my best to converse with them. In three months, I spoke enough English to hold a fairly intelligent conversation. Initially, I wondered about whether or not I would be dancing for a long time. I had made some friends, and for a while, I felt like I belonged.

I was swept off my feet by my newfound independence, I didn't even care that this type of work was viewed as "unsavory." I was living in a fantasyland. How strange that under such scandalous circumstance I found myself happy for the first time in my life. However, after a year of moving from place to place, I decided to live and work in one city, and surround myself with beautiful things, beautiful clothes, and a new car. When I was not working, I was shopping. At first, it felt good and seemed to fill the void within. However, this would only last as long as I kept spending. When I slowed down, I kind of saw a pattern beginning to develop, but there was little time between my shopping sprees and making money to realize the seriousness of my actions. I was always running, keeping myself busy—or should I say dizzy?—trying to kill the pain of loneliness. I never succumbed to the use of drugs or alcohol and was always in control of my actions. In fact, I enjoyed the power that came with it, helping girls who needed assistance. I gave them a place to stay, I listened to their pain, and I offered them advice. This became my way of justifying my place in the adult entertainment business. I felt I was making a difference in a deplorable world, and it made me feel better about myself. This was my excuse; I was helping others. I also made certain my family did not know about my secret life. I dressed, talked, and acted by society's rules. I was always respectable and presentable.

The first few years of dancing, I truly believed that money was what made me happy. Night after night, I danced, while in the day I showered myself with gifts. I believed I had it all. On the outside, I seemed happy and strong. However, no one knew how much I was covering up inside, not even me.

1986: Four years later

After years of entertaining in bars and dealing with men on a daily basis, I became very strong minded. As time equalled money, men were willing to pay for my company. I would sit smiling and talking about the same old thing night after night. Over the years, I met many nice men, some lonely and some with broken hearts like mine. I also met the married men who came for an occasional beer, just to look at the pretty girls. Of course, there were the occasional creeps; however, these men learned fast enough that they were wasting their time and their money with me. There were also the crazy fun-loving guys who came in groups to have a good time. They were the loudest and wildest of all men, and I could connect better with them. They were friendly and amusing, but I was there to make money and not to socialize. Nevertheless, one of those young men caught my attention one day. He had a lovely smile and a positive attitude; this caught my attention. In addition to his great personality, he was attractive and charming in every way.

During work, I often found myself looking for him. Whenever I could, I would spend time at his table. Strangely enough, I did not think about money when he was around. He would show up after work every Friday afternoon for a beer and sit at the same table with his friends. The second he walked through the doors, I lit up like a flame. However, these feelings scared me, as they wouldn't go away. I started thinking about him constantly, longing to be with him, trying hard not to fall under his spell, but never before had I felt this strongly about a man. I knew I could not allow myself to become emotionally involved with anyone; I was already involved with someone else. But it did not matter how I tried to stop it, I was falling head over heels in love with this man. His name was Luke. I was anticipating his arrival one Friday afternoon but he failed to show. I looked at his table and the empty chair and felt disappointed and hurt. This reaction was a revelation to me. I was in trouble big time! I could not function properly. All day, I caught myself looking at the front doors, hoping to see him enter. "Please show up," I kept repeating to myself.

The following Friday, I waited for him once more, but again he did not show and I did not see him the Friday after that either. I was heartbroken and my days seemed endless. I began to wonder if I would ever see him again. The disappearance of my secret love forced me to face my emotions head on.

What is happening to me? Can I really be in love? I wondered.

For months, I had been feeling this way, but had failed to act on it. I now realized how emotionally I was drawn to this man. In fact, my love had reached a level I could not fully understand.

Is this what true love is suppose to feel like? I thought. *Is he the love of my life? Will he ever walk through these doors again?*

I went to work on the following Friday with one thought only: *Will he be here today?* While getting ready, I found myself daydreaming about him, and consequently I arrived late for work. As I entered the club, I looked anxiously towards the back of the room, desperately hoping to see him there. He was!

Oh, my God, he looked so good. He had never looked that good before.

I was as numb as if I had been turned to stone and my legs seemed unable to carry me. I was incredibly embarrassed, as if the whole world could see my panic. I dragged myself into the washroom and cried uncontrollably. There was no turning back. I was definitely in love. All year, I had battled with my feelings, hoping that one day I would get over it; however, the love I felt for this man had only grown stronger. He had totally captured my heart.

During this time, I could not act on my feelings because I was with a man named Mark, whom I had planned on marrying. I was twenty-three years old and wanted to feel whole, thinking perhaps that a family would help me make sense of my life. More than anything else, I wanted a baby to love, and I knew Mark would be a great father. Mark never tried to change me in anyway, and often made me feel better about myself. Although Mark brought peace and stability into my life, I still felt that something was missing. Throughout the years we were together, I had tried my best to keep the relationship alive. However, I certainly had failed because my heart belonged to someone else. I could no longer continue in the relationship, and I had to tell Mark the truth. Breaking up with him was one of the hardest things I ever had to do. I felt guilty for years, it was never my intention to hurt him in anyway, but I did, and I am sorry.

I am truly sorry.

Luke was sitting at his usual table and I was in the washroom trying to pull myself together. After calming down and taking some deep breaths, I came out with a big smile on my face. We made eye contact; there was no doubt in my mind, Luke was the one for me. "Hello," I said shyly, wondering if he was as delighted to see me as I was to see him. Luke's friend was still sitting with us and I lost the courage to tell Luke how I felt. However, he must have known. It would have been impossible not to; this would have definitely let him know how I felt as I sat with him for over two hours. When eventually we were alone, I did something I had never done before. I ordered a drink, hoping that the sweet peach schnapps would calm my nerves. Still I could not bring myself to tell him how I felt, but we were without a doubt flirting with one another.

Luke left the club and I went back to work. It was Friday night and the boys were loud and crazy. Later that evening, however, I noticed the silhouette of a man sitting alone at the back of the club. Never in a million years did I expect it to be Luke. It was. He had changed clothes, fixed his hair, and looked ready to go out on a date. He had dressed to impress and he did! As I approached his table, I realized he was as nervous as I. I sat down and ordered another drink. This time, I knew why he had come back. My shift was ending and Luke suggested we go out for a bite to eat—of course, I accepted.

It was a calm spring night, the stars on the horizon sparkling above our heads. There was something strangely reassuring about that night. I was over the moon in love and light on my feet. I guess I was walking on air, because never had I felt this alive before. The gentle breeze seemed to move me toward Luke. I felt like a young girl on her first date, ready to be swept away by her prince charming. I had millions of butterflies in my stomach. As it was so late, we couldn't find a restaurant open, so Luke suggested a hotel restaurant; however we could only get a meal if we rented a room, which we did. I sat on the bed while Luke sat at the table next to it. We were alone and tension was growing between us, and the silence you could cut with a knife. It became very uncomfortable. My eyes were on the menu, but my thoughts were definitely not on the food. I looked up and Luke was looking at me. I smiled; I could see him clearly, as he sat right under the light. For a moment, I studied his face. I had never seen him in full light before. I took a moment to memorize his beautiful green eyes, perfect skin, and wonderful mouth. I wanted him to kiss me big time! Finally, Luke came and sat beside me and started asking questions about my family. As he looked into my eyes, I felt weak and embarrassed, and wanted desperately to escape the strange feelings I had. I decided to take a shower. I needed time to think. I was amazed at his self-control; he never made a move toward me. After I had showered, I sat beside him. Luke remembered I had complained about my back aching, so he offered to massage it for me. I removed my shirt and lay down on my stomach. He placed his hands on my shoulders, softly caressing my skin, massaging tenderly for some time, and then, he began to rub down my back, firmly moving up and down my spine. As his fingers caressed my neck, I felt his breath on my face and could feel his heartbeat; I turned my head to place my lips on his and kissed him tenderly. A shiver of delight ran down my spine; I was overwhelmed by desire. He gently turned me over and pressed his body against mine, a fire igniting between us. I shall leave you to imagine what else happened on that star-filled night.

    We couldn't stand being apart, so three months later, we moved in together. I knew without a doubt Luke was the love of my life, and Luke felt the same way about me. I was twenty-three years old and knew in my heart I had found my soul mate. Six months later, I was pregnant.

Chapter Four
SWEET JESSY

1988

I was eight months pregnant, and we were extremely happy. I had stopped working two months into my pregnancy. I spent all of my time cheerfully shopping for baby things, and decorating the baby's room. I loved my life. I had the man of my dreams and was about to become a mother. I didn't care that I had gained fifty-two pounds. I had a marvellous reason for the extra weight that I had gained. There was a little miracle living and growing inside me, our baby. Through our love, Luke and I had created a life, and we were just a few weeks away from sharing our beautiful baby with the world.

However, on August 3, I came home from my regular monthly checkup with concerns. Our son was to arrive very soon; I felt ready to explode. My doctor had made an appointment for me to see a specialist at Sick Children's Hospital. He was worried I had retained too much water around the placenta. He said I had grown too big, too quickly, within the last week. I had an appointment for a fetal echocardiogram, along with a detailed ultrasound for the baby's kidneys. I had already had numerous ultrasounds as I had been told our baby Jessy was missing a kidney. Luke was by my side, and doctors and nurses were rushing in and out of the room, staring at the screen while talking quietly amongst themselves. The room quickly became crowded and I was overwhelmed. There was tension in the air, and fear and uncertainty, and my mind pictured the most horrible scenarios. I was desperately holding on to hope that everything was okay, but the waiting drove me crazy. No one explained what was happening. They would just converse in medical terms while completely ignoring me. The nurse then asked Luke to leave the room, and my poor love walked away and sat in the waiting room alone to anticipate the worst moment of his life. He must have been out of his mind with worry. For me, I desperately needed him by my side for his support and for my sanity. Time passed slowly; the nurses and specialists still would not answer any of my questions. It did not matter whom I spoke to, their response was the same: "Just be patient a little longer."

Hours had passed, still with no information or the least bit of consideration, and absolutely no compassion. I sunk into despair.

Can anyone notice the distress I'm in? I thought. *I'm scared sick and I need some relief.*

Can anyone help me? I cried inside.

Between examinations, I was left alone with my frightening thoughts, and my brain was screaming for answers. *Please give me something to calm my nerves,* I thought to myself. But everyone ignored my tears, until finally a nurse calmly asked me to get dressed, saying, "You and your husband have a meeting with a specialist in a private room." Time stood still. I was just about to lose it when Luke entered the room. I grabbed his arm as if he was my savior and I depended on his strength to get me through it. Even though things did not look good, I made a great effort to trust that everything would be all right. Luke managed to give me a crooked smile, hoping to provide some type of encouragement, although I could see fear in his sad eyes. The specialist avoided me, turning directly toward Luke and telling him what they had discovered. "Your baby has hydronephrosis, which is an abnormality in his remaining kidney. We also detected an abnormality in your baby's heart. Unfortunately, your son has congenital heart disease." Then he added, "I am very sorry to tell you, your baby is very very sick."

Oh, my God! This is not happening. I thought in distress. *I must be dreaming. Wake up, Nancy. WAKE UP, for God's sake! Jessy is fine. We are fine. We have to be fine.*

I was in so much pain, I grabbed my head and begged God to help me.

Please, make it stop! Please make it stop! My mind did not want to stop. *I can't breathe. Please help me!* I screamed to God.

I collapsed into Luke's arms, hoping to drown my sorrows in his chest, and refused to hear anymore of this nonsense. However, my cry for help was not answered.

Tears were streaming down my face; I felt as if I had been torn apart; this could not be happening. "Can you do something? Please do something," I asked the specialist.

"I'm sorry," was all the doctor said to us.

What is happening to our dream, to my perfect life? I thought.

My mind was screaming, *Why, why, why ...* I had eaten the right food, I had taken plenty of milk, I also took the right vitamins, and walked every day, and read books about having a healthy pregnancy. "So WHY is this happening to us?" I cried.

"What are you saying? Is my baby going to survive all this?" I asked fearfully.

"I'm sorry to tell you, but your baby will not survive," the doctor said. "Your son will die within a few hours following his birth. Your baby cannot live without being attached to you. The moment his umbilical cord is cut, your baby will slowly pass on. I am so sorry," he again repeated.

Oh, my God, CAN SOMEBODY WAKE ME UP! "I don't have the strength to go through this.

Furthermore, the specialist informed us that I had to carry the baby to full term.

How can I continue to term knowing that it is all a lie? I thought desperately. *How can I go on, knowing that my son will soon die? I don't want any of this. What I want is my family, my son. Instead all I got is pain, TERRIBLE PAIN. What about Luke, how is he going to survive all this? How are we going to survive it all?*

We left the hospital, and I cried with despair for the entire ride home, hitting the dashboard with my fists and kicking the door with my foot—I wanted out, out of this nightmare. I hadn't asked for this, so why was it happening? My life was not supposed to go this way. It was supposed to be a fairy tale, a happy story. Luke drove silently in shock and disbelief all the way home. No words came out of his mouth; this I found irritated me. I wanted him to scream, to swear, to cry, TO GET MAD, but no, he was numb; he drove home without a sound. When we arrived home, the phone would not stop ringing. My family and friends knew about the appointment at Sick Children's Hospital and wanted to know what had happened. Luke answered the phone and gave them the terrible news. They of course asked to speak with me, but I did not want to talk to anyone. They were genuinely concerned about me, but I just wanted to be left alone.

Every day Jessy was kicking in my stomach and I suffered every minute of every day. Whenever he moved, it reminded me that soon he would die. Feeling him move was emotionally painful and yet it was also a miracle, but this little miracle would soon be over. Every night I struggled to fall asleep, and when I opened my eyes, the nightmare began all over again.

Oh, God, is this true? Where did I go wrong? Is this a punishment? Is this karma? What did I do to deserve this horrible pain? Why me? Why this? Why? Why? Why?

Then I thought, *Maybe they've made a mistake, maybe there is still hope. Doctors are not God. They make mistakes. There must be something they can do to help my son, surgery perhaps.* I was so confused and frustrated. One minute I wanted Jessy out, and the next, I wanted to keep him inside me forever. However, it became clear to me that I should no longer be pregnant, and so I wanted him out. The next day, I went to see my doctor and demanded to be induced. On July 26, the specialist prepared the hospital staff for my arrival at Women's College Hospital. Going through labor is a major challenge in itself, and now going through it in the state that I was in made it devastating. The contractions had grown closer and closer together and the pain became unbearable. The doctor injected a shot of morphine on each side of my hips and gave me the epidural; eventually all physical pain stopped. After sixteen hours of labor, my sweet baby boy was born. The moment the nurse placed Jessy in my arms, I didn't know if I should feel joy or grief. My son was perfect; he had all his tiny toes and fingers, and he weighed six pounds and nine ounces. From what I could see, I was convinced that the doctor had made a huge mistake. However, he still told us Jessy would soon pass away. But my son was not going to die. I wouldn't let him. All of a sudden Jessy's little feet and fingers turned blue. Oh, God, I was witnessing my son fading away. With very little time left, I had to do something. I pleaded and cried and demanded to give my son one more chance; they had to look at his heart once again.

During the second round of tests, friends and family came to visit us and a wave of cold fear penetrated my insides as the specialist entered the room. He asked everyone to leave. "Don't get me wrong," the expert said. "Your son is very sick but the specialist who had done the echocardiogram had misdiagnosed your son's heart condition; the problem with your son's heart is that the right and left ventricle are reversed and ..." He continued with the medical terms while my mind was bombarded with words that I had never heard before. I asked myself, *Is there hope in his diagnosis?*

"If your son survives his heart surgery, he will probably have to go through another heart operation in his lifetime. In addition to that, Jessy will have to undergo surgery for correcting the condition of his remaining kidney, and possibly a kidney transplant. Sadly, your son will go through many surgeries in his young life. Nonetheless, your son now has a chance of survival."

Oh, God, there is hope! I screamed to myself.

The minute chance of survival the doctors gave my son did not fully register with me. I only knew there was hope, a chance of a miracle. Jessy was transferred to Sick Children's Hospital, and since the two hospitals were only a few blocks apart, Luke gladly pushed my wheelchair along the streets of Toronto so we could be with Jessy. Our first visit to Sick Children's Hospital was terrifying, as we did not expect to see so much suffering. My sweet baby boy was plugged into all kinds of machines. His arms were stretched in a T position and his legs were wide apart, with nothing covering his naked body. He had tubes coming out of his nose, skull, penis, and arm. He was exposed for the whole world to see his pain. At that moment I questioned my decision to try to save him. The nurse and specialist tried to convince us that Jessy was not suffering, but it was hard to believe.

I prayed silently, *God, I don't want to make this decision. I want you to tell me what to do. Should I sign the consent papers?* I questioned. *Am I picking the right battle for my son to undertake? Should I keep fighting for him?* I didn't know.

Jessy survived his first surgery, but could no longer urinate through his penis. This was disheartening and terrifying.

> *Dear God,*
> *I am willing to let my son go if it's what you want. However, give us the strength to go through it without too much pain. Grant me the courage to see what needs to be done, and please explain to me what I need to*

know quickly so this nightmare can end. If by any chance I am dreaming, please wake me up, as I am about to lose my mind. I'm begging and pleading with you, God, please help me to make the right decision.

I had to consider the possibilities. I had to believe in miracles. I just had to. I could not have lived with myself knowing that I hadn't tried to do everything I possibly could.

I believed the misdiagnosis of Jessy's heart condition had to be a sign, an indication that my son would survive, and so I kept hoping and believing. Still, I needed someone on my side, someone who could recognize the difficult position I was in, someone who would tell me that I was doing the right thing, as I felt so alone.

If I want this bad enough, will I have my son in my life? Will I have my "happy ever after" family? I cried, praying to God.

Three days later, the specialist informed us that Jessy's heart was weakening, "Your son needs heart surgery as soon as possible." Once again, we were asked to sign consent forms, and, unable to make the decision, I hesitated. I cried desperately in the waiting room. This time Luke did not even try to convince me to let Jessy go. He took it on himself to sign the forms. Did he sign the papers to release me from the enormous responsibility? Or did he sign because he had changed his mind? I still don't know.

I had never seen Luke pray in his life, but he prayed now.

Together, we prayed!

During the excruciating wait, I heard two voices in my head, the one of hope and the one of terror. It felt like a curse, until finally, the heart surgeon walked into the waiting room, and she seemed pleased that the surgery was successful. However, my son was only ten days old and already marked for life.

Surprisingly, Jessy recovered from his surgery quite well, and three days following his heart surgery, I held him in my arms. A few days later, I was able to feed him, bathe him, and rock him to sleep. I whispered in his ear every minute, telling him how much I loved him. It was the happiest day of my life. Every little step we were taking together became a reassurance that soon my son would be coming home. Every little thing mothers do for their babies, I was doing. Finally, I had become a mother, Jessy's mother.

"Sweet little one, I wish I knew you better," I whispered.

As Jessy's parents, we were responsible for his well-being, and we were supposed to make the right choices in his life. He depended on our ability to do the right thing. Making the decision for him was dreadfully difficult. I wished he could have contacted us in some way to let us know what he wanted us to do.

The specialist assured us repeatedly that Jessy would be ready to go home soon. But was he really, I wondered.

How can they be sure? Jessy looked so fragile to us.

On August 10, trusting that my son was in good hands, I decided to go home and get a good night's sleep. At 5:00 a.m. the phone rang. I woke up terrified. Luke picked up the phone and from the look on his face, I panicked. "You and your wife have to come to the hospital right away," the nurse said. The thirty-minute drive to the hospital felt like an eternity. I was crying, "Drive faster, drive faster. FASTER! I shouted. Poor Luke, he was driving as fast as he could, but it was not fast enough for me. I needed to be there immediately. I could not stop trembling, nothing made any sense, nothing seemed real to me. It could not be the end, not after all the misery and pain. As we rushed to be by Jessy's side, I came face to face with a woman whose baby shared the room with my son. She was sitting beside the door and seemed to be waiting for someone. When I first opened the door, I realized the two babies who shared the room with Jessy were gone, and their mothers had vanished as well. However, there was one mother sitting outside the room crying. I wondered why.

While holding Jessy in my arms, I was presented with the worst fear a mother can bear. In that moment, my whole world was shattered and my entire life story shifted. Unwillingly, I found myself on a different journey, riding on waves of terrifying pain.

When you watch your dreams crumble to bits and can do nothing about it, it's hard or even impossible to see the lessons that the experience can bring. It can take us months or years, if we are willing to let go of the pain and anger, before we can see the great learning opportunity that such an experience can give us.

Reality hit me like a blade through my heart.

My son was lifeless.

This couldn't be happening. Life cannot be this cruel. Surely, I thought, God cannot be that hurtful.

Is this truly happening? Has my son gone? Sweet Jessy, I'm sorry. I'm so sorry.

My poor husband stood beside me in shock. The nurse came rushing in and tried to take Jessy from my arms. I pushed her away saying, "Go away. Leave us alone!" She left, but quickly returned with the doctor. "You are not supposed to be here; you were supposed to meet me in my office," the specialist said.

"What happened?" I asked him. "Was he alone or was there someone with him? Oh, God, it should have been me with him. I should have been here all along!" I cried. What happened?" I asked again.

"Your baby's heart simply gave up," he answered.

Oh, God, we shouldn't have signed the consent papers. We should have let him go peacefully. Luke was right. I should have listened to him, I thought.

I held my son in my arms, loving him with all my heart. Luke also held him, gently touching his fingers, silently saying good-bye.

This dreadful morning of August 11 has never left me. The thought that I should have slept at the hospital that night has haunted me for fourteen years. It was the biggest regret of my life, and I could not let it go.

I gently put Jessy back into his crib and left the room. As we left the hospital, I noticed a woman sitting on a chair by the elevator. She was the mother who had been crying earlier outside Jessy's room. *Is she there purposely to see me?* I wondered. *Is she waiting for me?*

She looked at me and told me, "Jessy cried all night and no one came to see him. After a while, I picked him up and tried to rock him to sleep, but he would not stop crying. I held him and stayed with him while he cried all night, when all of a sudden, he just went quiet. I thought he had fallen asleep," she softly said.

"Oh, my God." I felt so guilty. Now that her words were stabbing me in the heart, I was hit by extreme remorse. I felt mentally, physically, and emotionally sick. I thought I was the worst mother in the world. I wanted to scream; she had made me feel even worse if that was possible. I knew that she did not mean to, but her words tortured me. I had been a mother only for fifteen days and had failed miserably. It was my responsibility to make sure that my son was in safe hands. I should have been there attending to his needs. It should have been me comforting him. He should have died in my arms.

Today's reflection

Every earthly struggle has within it the potential to move us to a higher place. Challenges hold within them the opportunity to transform our lives, to push us on to a higher purpose, if we are willing to let go and grow from them. All of us can be knocked down at some point in our lives, one way or another; however, we have to decide whether or not to get back up. We need time to heal, but when we are ready, and if we make that choice, we can look beyond the pain and use the experience to improve our lives.

Today I want to remember my son Jessy by his gentle touch, his warm skin, his beautiful face, his piercing green eyes, and his wonderful smell. I want to remember him exactly like the first time I held him in my arms. This memory of a sweet angel brings peace to my heart.

To The Mother Who Held My Son

To the mother who held my son and comforted him, who was with him in his last moments, I want to thank you from the bottom of my heart. I am so grateful for the time, touch, and compassion you gave my son. I will never forget your kindness. I thank you so very much.

My nights were unbearable, filled with remorse. I was feeling responsible for Jessy's pain and suffering, and I was unable to get out of bed for many days following his death. I drove myself crazy thinking of what I should or should *not* have done. I sank into a deep depression. "Please, God, explain to me why I have to go through so much pain, and why I feel abandoned and alone every second of my life," I cried.

Luke and I flew to Fort Lauderdale, Florida, hoping to find some kind of peace. But the grieving process takes time, weeks, months, even years; it cannot be fast-tracked. I was in too much of a rush to feel better; I just couldn't stand the pain. I felt more hopeless day after day. Even the calm of the ocean could not ease the pain in my heart, and my mind began to play tricks on me. My emptiness brought with it the intense fear of losing Luke, the love of my life. The thought of losing Luke was not about him leaving, it was the thought that he too might die. I was unaware of what I was doing to myself. The feeling grew to a level that caused me extreme anxiety for months.

On my return from Florida, the room I had prepared for Jessy seemed strangely different. I looked around and yet nothing had changed, so I sat on the floor, engulfed in deep sadness. I opened every drawer of Jessy's dresser, smelling each piece of clothing that I had washed in Ivory Snow. The scent penetrated every cell of my body and I cried.

As I opened the last drawer, a chill went through me. Inside was a tiny box. Oh, God, I knew exactly what was in it. Attached to the precious little box was a small envelope with a small stuffed animal and Jessy's hospital bracelet. I took hold of the little box and held it close to my heart. I could not believe what I was holding in my arms. "Jessy, I miss you so very much."

Luke had asked his mother to take care of Jessy's cremation, and she had placed his ashes in his room. This was devastating and yet I found myself embracing the little package. When Luke went back to work, I was left alone with my imagination. I sat in Jessy's room and felt in my heart there was no reason to go on. I would continually get bad headaches from obsessing about what had happened to Jessy. I would tell myself I was responsible for my son's suffering and that I was a bad mother. I felt that this horrible ordeal was a way of punishing me for my past mistakes, and a hard life was probably going to be my sentence. I told myself so many crazy things. Sometimes I was under such stress that I felt I was indeed losing it. To escape from the pain, I returned to my old habit of working and shopping. It was my way of coping with the worst experience of my life. My mother kept calling me, as she wanted us to bury Jessy in Québec City. However, I was now too attached to the little box to let it go.

The club quickly became my shelter. Work was a place I could temporarily escape my feelings, where I could stop thinking about everything. Nonetheless, this kept me chained at the club. I became more comfortable with the people at work than I did with my own family and friends. At times, I felt there must be a greater purpose in life for me. Surely, this could not be all there is to it. Slowly I began to feel how unfulfilling a purely material life really was. I was forced to look for a deeper meaning, and there were many signs for this awakening to take place, but I was stubborn. There was a big part of me that refused to change, therefore refusing to grow. My years of materialism left me totally empty. I had not grown intellectually, or emotionally, or spiritually. I was trapped in my isolated mind. I existed only to work and shop. Sadly, I had forgotten how to enjoy life, how to have fun. Escaping my feelings was a choice, although an unconscious one, but still it was a choice, and clearly did not heal my broken heart. In fact, it had made things much worse.

I had to wake up!

Unfortunately, I still believed that money was the answer to all my troubles. Thinking happiness could be obtained with money and power was such an illusion. When I first started dancing, the money and admiration I received brought with it feelings I had never experienced before, but these feelings gave me a *false* sense of self-esteem, security, and power. For many years, my self-worth had been in the hands of men who reacted favourably towards me. As long as I was in demand, my self-esteem stayed intact. Even though I knew something was not right with me, I kept doing the same old thing, dancing for money. I never went back to school. In fact, I lived in my own little world, my own comfort zone, where I believed I was safe. I never stopped to question my behavior or lifestyle. I was not at all ready to wake up. My twenties were very much about surviving. I became so good at covering up the pain that it was impossible for my friends and family to really know me. Everyone assumed that I was fine. They hadn't a clue how I truly felt inside. I was searching for something to fill the emptiness in my heart and I truly believed that a baby would fill that void.

Time healed some of my wounds and work helped hide my loneliness. However, my suffering had only hibernated, because the deep sadness (soul-pain) would one day awaken to make my life a living hell.

Today's reflection

As a young child, I believed in God, even during the tough separations from my family. I knew of God's existence, I sensed His presence in the dark of night. God was there during the toughest time in my youth. I would pray in bed and He would be there listening. I would feel safe and protected. However, since Jessy's death, something had changed. I had lost my faith.

Two years after his death, my mother convinced me to bury Jessy at St-Hélene Comté de Bagot, where I lived during my infant years. My grandparents had purchased a plot at that cemetery and wanted to have Jessy by their side. My grandmother, who was always afraid of dying, had told my mother that since Jessy passed away, her fear of dying had left her. She believed Jessy was an angel who would meet her when she was ready to go. I knew then it was the right time and the right place for Jessy to rest in peace.

Jessy was buried in the summer of 1990. For many years, my grandparents took flowers to his grave until the day they eventually joined him.

My sweet dearest angel,
God knows how I tried.
I think of your height,
I think of your eyes.

God promised me days,
devoid of all pain.
Days without sorrow,
days without rain.

Days full of laughter,
days full of joy.
Wait for me on high,
my sweet baby boy.

—Mom

My dream to become a mother became an obsession with me. A few months following Jessy's death, I started talking about adoption. I guess I was in a hurry to fill the void in my heart.

Luke and I were married on September 24, 1988, at City Hall. It was a quick ceremony and we immediately applied for adoption in two countries, Mexico and Colombia. Mexico refused our request and Colombia sent us a two-page application form in Spanish, which included many rules and regulations. We were completely overwhelmed. Luke suggested we try to get pregnant again, and ten months later, I was expecting. This was wonderful news.

In the summer of 1990, I was beautifully round with child. I had stopped working and spent my time daydreaming, and by Christmas, I had gained forty-five pounds. I was healthy, happy, and very pregnant. I felt blessed to have another chance to become a mother. However, in the early months of my pregnancy, my doctor wanted to play it safe and learn the condition of the baby's heart and kidneys. Each time the test came back normal, and each time it was a celebration. February 11, 1990, we welcomed into the world our second baby boy, Tyeson Sean Demets, so loved and beautiful, and on Valentine's Day, we brought our little bundle of joy home.

Two years later, in September 1992, I received the good news that I was pregnant again. However, I was often sick with flu and nausea and I ended up spending the first six months of my pregnancy in bed. I was glad when labor started two weeks prematurely. I had gained fifty-eight pounds and was extremely uncomfortable. On May 8, 1993, we welcomed our third baby boy, Spencer Lucas Demets. Spencer was perfect, with dark hair, dark brown eyes, and light tanned skin. His brother Tyeson was born with blond hair, hazel eyes, and light skin, and remains so to this day. They were completely opposite in looks, and time revealed how different my children are personality wise.

While I held and kissed my newborn son in the hospital, all of a sudden I noticed a change in his breathing. Spencer was having difficulty. I panicked and screamed for help and in a flash, a nurse rushed my baby out of the room. The past came flooding back to shake my world again and plunge me into darkness. Overwhelmed by the bad memories, I hurt to the very core of my being. Luke had left the hospital to be with Tyeson, and I was alone, panicking. The wait was unbearable. I called home, and my friend Sasha who had been taking care of Tyeson picked up the phone.

"It's happening all over again," I cried to Sasha. "Spencer is not doing well. He is struggling for breath. It does not look good. Why is this happening AGAIN?" I yelled.

"WHY, SASHA?" I screamed once again. Poor Sasha, I almost deafened her with my screaming. I eventually calmed down, but not until I let it all out.

"I need Luke. Where is he?" I said. Luke had not yet arrived home from the hospital. I hung up the phone and rushed back to the

Intensive Care Unit. The moment Luke arrived home, Sasha gave him the terrible news. He immediately returned to the hospital to find Spencer plugged into a heart monitor. The echocardiogram and ultrasounds done during the pregnancy had showed that Spencer had two healthy kidneys and that his heart was in good health. So what was the problem?

Why the emergency?

The nurse asked that we wait in my room for the specialist. Luke tried to comfort me, but my horrific thoughts were overwhelming. I could not believe what we were going through again. I stood in front of the window and cried to God.

"If there is a God in this freaking life, this is the time to prove it. PLEASE DO SOMETHING. Please, please, please do something."

My heart had been broken so many times, I didn't know if I could survive another loss. "Please, God, give my son a chance."

Once more, my life was being ripped apart; to bring happiness into my life seemed to be a constant struggle.

I read somewhere that God never gives us more than we can bear.

"God, is that true?" I questioned.

Finally, the specialist entered the room, "Three doctors have examined your son and we all agree. Your baby has a very small hole in his heart ..."

I immediately panicked. "Not his heart," I shouted. "Not again."

"Spencer's condition is nothing like the condition of your firstborn. Spencer has two healthy kidneys and a healthy heart. The hole in your son's heart will probably close on its own. We have seen this happen many times before. It is not a critical condition at this time. We will keep Spencer in the ICU for forty-eight hours to monitor his heart and then we will test him once again."

A journey to self-acceptance – A message of hope, love and courage.

"NO MORE WAITING. Please don't make me wait," I cried.

I've waited all my life. I waited for my parents to reconcile. I waited for my mother's return. I waited to be reunited with my sisters. I waited for the hurt to stop. I waited for God to answer my prayers. I waited for Jessy to get better. I waited to become a mother. I waited to be happy, and now I am waiting again. I am sick and tired of waiting," I thought to myself.

The waiting felt to me like a life sentence, but I had no choice, I had to wait another forty-eight hours. I had no more tears left; I was exhausted. I had just delivered my baby and had not had time to recover. The nurse wanted to give me something to help me sleep, but I refused it. I had to be awake, I just had to. I could not miss a moment of my son's life. Spencer had to know that I was here no matter what. I drove the nurses crazy. I watched Spencer like a hawk, and if I saw something change, I immediately called for help. The nurse would tell me the same thing over and over. "Spencer is fine. The heart monitor would beep if Spencer were in trouble. Relax and go to sleep." Too many bad memories made me act this way. I was so full of fear and regret. I had lost all my trust in God, doctors, and everyone else years ago.

The wait felt endless, but eventually the time passed and Spencer was no longer attached to the heart monitor. The specialist informed us that whatever they had seen two days ago was now gone. Spencer's heart had healed on its own, just as they had expected.

We took Spencer home on Mother's Day, May 10, 1993. I was thirty years old, and I wept with joy. I had received the greatest gift a mother could get—a healthy baby and a happy family.

My friend Sasha stayed with us a few more days and Spencer slept with her. I tried to recuperate, but I was terribly anxious. I felt Spencer was only safe with me. I would wait to hear him cry to ease my anxieties. Spencer woke up every two hours and I remember praying for that moment to arrive. When Sasha left to go home, Spencer slept with me, but I was too fearful to sleep. I watched him breathing like a crazy obsessed fool. I slept with my hand on his stomach, making sure he was still breathing. Every now and then I sat up in a panic, putting my face close to his mouth so I could feel his breath, as if I needed to taste it. Some days were worse than others; nonetheless, I carried on this way for months. I soon became completely exhausted. Accepting the fact that Spencer's heart was okay took a great deal of time. However, the fear of losing another child never left me; it had become a fixation.

When Spencer was a toddler, I lived through many paranoid moments with his health. What's more, Spencer would wake up three to four times a night, crying for his pacifier or for a gentle touch from me. Weekdays, I was a super mom. I never slept more than four hours a day. On weekends Luke helped, but Spencer and Tyeson always wanted Mommy. The pressure I inflicted on myself was beginning to take its toll. My fear and lack of trust made me do things that a sane person would never have done. When the time came for Tyeson to go to school, I was forced to find ways to ease my fears. I trusted no one with my children, certainly not the bus driver. Tyeson was a big boy now and wanted to take the school bus. Afraid that my son was in danger without me, I put Spencer in his car seat and followed the bus to school. On one occasion, Tyeson waved at us. I could not believe it. He had known all along that we were there. When Tyeson arrived home that day, he asked, "Why are you following the bus, Mommy? I know you are. Why don't you drive me to school then?" I felt stupid and insecure but I could not tell him. I needed the peace of mind, and I did whatever I needed to do to feel better and to alleviate my fears.

Sometimes I would be in such a panic that I would drive to Tyeson's school, walk around the building and standing outside, I would look through the windows to reassure myself that he was there. Later, when it was time for Spencer to go to school, I found out that I could become a school volunteer, which I did for five years. This helped with my insecurities.

A journey to self-acceptance – A message of hope, love and courage.

I lived in fear, doubt, distrust, and panic for most of my children's lives. I slept very little, rested very little, and worried constantly and so for years I was like a zombie. I could not stop obsessing over my children. I had become trapped in a vicious cycle, and I did not realize how destructive my behavior had become. I was unaware I needed help. I believed that everything was fine, but I was slowly dying inside. I never realized my actions and lack of self-care would have such detrimental consequences. I was burning the candle at both ends, and life was about to send me a huge wake-up call.

Before we can undo any damage and create ourselves anew, it is critical to take a good look at our lives to see where we can make healthy changes. However, we have to be aware in order for this to happen!

At the root of my behavior lived the basic egoic patterns—the unconsciousness, the emotional pain, the need to be right, and the mental noises that persisted obsessively. I had become an over-doer and a perfectionist who allowed NO mistakes or breaks. I tried to control my children's existence twenty-four/seven. I felt safe only when my children were close by. Never would I want them to move away from me. I was like a watchdog, always on high alert. I lived with ideas and beliefs based on danger. I lost myself in the extreme demands and acute stress that I persistently put myself in. This behavior was beginning to fry my brain and my body was about to give up. After years of suppressing my emotions and working as a watchdog, I became seriously ill.

All along, I had been an active, although unconscious participant, in the creation of this story. Unfortunately, I did not recognize that the tired skinny me was the reflection of my obsession, and the exhaustion came from my emotional state of mind. It was time to get beyond the tears and be brutally honest with myself. I had to stop.

But how? I didn't even realize what I was doing. I was trying to survive by suppressing my tears and fears and was too stubborn to admit that I needed help. I was striving to maintain a perfectly normal appearance to the outside world—in fact, I think this is what I have been doing all my life. Healing could only take place if I stopped doing and started *being*. I had to make peace with my pain.

But how? Life had sent me many signs to stop, yet I was not aware of the messages—the Whispers of the Universe. The noises in my head made it impossible for me to hear them. It was time to snap out of this unconscious state and wake up!

But I was a slow learner. For a few more years, I kept on doing what I always did, and guess what? I got more fatigued, and had more headaches, and became more stressed, and I even loss more weight. I was not aware enough to make changes in my life. I lived in constant dread and anxiety.

Sasha would sometimes ask to take the boys for a weekend, but I would come up with excuses to refuse her offers. On one occasion, sick with a terrible cold, I considered separating myself from my children for two days. I let my children go with their godmother Sasha. Tyeson was five and Spencer was two. I looked forward to the rest. It was a chance to recuperate, and if I was lucky, a chance to spend time alone with my husband. Instead, however, a war started inside me. I started battling with my fears and worries. I created all kinds of mental pictures that soon made me psychologically sick. Even with my best friend, I felt that my children were in danger. I was not afraid that she would hurt them, but I imagined house fires, car accidents, kidnappings, falls, cuts, all kinds of danger, more and more danger.

While waiting for my children to come home, I put myself right into the terror zone. I made a promise that I would never let my children out of my sight again.

What was wrong with me? Who in her right mind would create scenarios so terrifying about her children? Who was crazy enough to do this to themselves?

Unfortunately, I was.

An update on Spencer's condition

Throughout his young years, Spencer's heart was tested and we were shocked to learn that a tiny hole in his heart was still a problem. At the age of ten, however, the hole had mysteriously disappeared. Then we were told Spencer had an unusually enlarged artery in his heart. At first we were worried, but we soon learned Spencer could live a successful and normal life without surgery. Spencer is now seventeen years old and the abnormal artery has not grown.

My son Spencer loves life. He has more energy than my whole family put together. He runs around like a little maniac. He loves sports, soccer, football, basketball, and he also enjoys jogging. He is so physically and mentally fit, we have no doubt Spencer will live a long and healthy life.

Following Spencer's heart diagnoses, my family doctor suggested that I have an echocardiogram and an ultrasound to look at my kidneys and heart. My kidneys were fine, but they detected a small hole in my heart. I could not believe it. I had lived my entire life with this condition without even knowing it. A couple of years later I was tested again and no signs of the tiny hole in my heart were found. What was that? Another miracle? Or is it something that happens frequently?

Chapter Five
THE INCESSANT DIALOGUE

Save me from my mind and love me from inside.

I'm certainly not alone suffering from depression, anxiety, and looking for the meaning of existence.

Please read through the next chapter quickly, as there is a lot of pain in these pages. I'm writing directly from my journal so you will know exactly how I felt during those terrible months of my life. Remember, however, I am not in that place anymore.

December 14, 1999—Thirty-six years old

Dear diary, it has been a while since I have written and I'm very sorry about that, but for the past seven months, I have been feeling so bad that I didn't have the courage or anything good to say, so I didn't write. I still don't have anything good to say, but I need to express my feelings. I don't know what is with me, I'm feeling afraid and terribly nervous. This type of nervousness is beyond my understanding. I can't rest physically or mentally; in fact, I can't stand being me.

A few weeks ago I went to see my family doctor, and I let him know how awful I feel every day. I have no energy and everything is overwhelming to me. The kids drive me crazy and I'm very impatient. I don't like it. My doctor suggested bed rest. He prescribed some medication for the anxiety and said to take it when I need it. "It will help," he said.

But I don't want to take anything.

January 8, 2000

Just before Christmas, I had eye surgery (to correct my vision) and everything went fine. So why am I still feeling panic? I still have the fear that something bad is about to happen. I feel sad and dragged down, and I don't know why. I don't understand this overwhelming anxiety that I feel every day. The frightening thoughts about my children also include me now; I constantly feel I am in danger and that something bad is going to happen.

I feel trapped. I want out.

Please, can't somebody help me!

I don't want to talk about it anymore.

January 15, 2000

I can't sleep. I can't eat. I'm losing so much weight and I fear the worst. The kids are so loud, I can't stand to be around them. What is happening to me? I don't recognize myself. Whenever I look at myself in the mirror, I see only ugliness. I look like a skeleton. I look like I have aged ten years. Everybody talks about my weight loss but there is nothing I can do about it. I just can't eat. I went to see my doctor again. He still says that it's stress-related and that I need to rest. "It will pass," he says. I don't think so! This feeling in my gut is much more then stress.

My mind thinks, thinks and thinks ... IT CANNOT STOP THINKING. It's driving me insane. I'm afraid of losing my sanity, my family, my life.

PLEASE, CAN SOMEONE HELP ME!

I cry every night, Luke doesn't know why, he doesn't understand what is happening. He has never seen me like this before. No one knows how much I'm suffering inside. No one can understand it, because no one can see what is torturing me. I can't even see it myself.

I'm afraid. I'm so afraid.

I'm terrified that I will completely lose it one day.

Am I going crazy?

AM I?

Everything bothers me. Noises amplify my anxiety. I can't even watch television because it's too fast, too loud, too negative, and it causes me to feel more anxious. From the moment I wake up to the moment I fall asleep, my thoughts are fanatical. I don't know why my mind does this and I don't know how to stop it. I feel that I am a prisoner in my own mind. Every part of my life is under attack.

Oh, God, am I crazy?

It hurts so badly.

PLEASE, MAKE IT STOP!

Please, make it stop.

January 30, 2000

It's two o'clock in the morning and I just endured another scary episode. I'm writing and my hand is still trembling from the terror. My mind does not want to SHUT UP! I cannot escape from it. I cannot make it stop. Please, make it stop.

PLEASE, LET ME OUT. Let me see the light.

Let me see my way out. I just can't take it any more.

PLEASE, QUIET MY MIND!

It's so noisy in here, it drives me mad.

Whenever I feel overpowered by all this dread and anxiety, my insides are on fire as if a volcano is about to erupt, and I feel a burning sensation running through my veins. It feels as if my blood is boiling, and during these attacks, I lose complete control of myself. The severity of heat and tension that I experience pushes the burning sensation down through my intestines, resulting in a sudden attack of diarrhea and a need to vomit. My heart beats so fast that it feels like it is about to burst out of my chest. When I have an attack, I'm so terrified that I want to run as fast as I can, but I don't know where to or why. I just want to run, but from WHAT?

Am I crazy?

Is there anyone in this freaking world going through this?

Am I alone with this?

I feel so alone.

February 2, 2000

Oh, God, I'm such a horrible mother.
I'm sorry. I'm so sorry.
Why do I have to be like this?
Is this day ever going to end?
I need to end all this suffering.
Yet I don't really want to die.
PLEASE HELP ME.
GET ME OUT OF THIS MISERY.
If nobody can help … what I am going to do?

Even pretending is hard. I don't have the strength or desire to see anyone. I don't want anybody to see how lost I am, so I hide from everyone. Luke wants me to call my mom but I don't want to. Now my kids feel that something is wrong with me because Luke keeps saying, "Stop it, boys, Mommy is sick, she doesn't feel good today, leave her alone." I'm trying my best to be normal around them, but I just can't manage their demands or their energy. It is just too much for me. I live mostly in my bedroom. I went to see my doctor again. This time he prescribed antidepressants. He still thinks that I'm over-stressed, "A burnout," he says. I think that I will take them tonight. I'm scared but I need help. I need a break.

I'm hoping that this medication will work tonight.
Make it work. Please make it work.

February 5, 2000

I have been taking these antidepressants for three days now and I didn't feel anything until last night. I took the antidepressant before bed and something horrific happened in the middle of the night. I woke up extremely nervous and scared out of my mind, as if the house was on fire or something bad had happened. I wanted to get out of the panic but my body was trapped in the terror. My arms felt numb. My legs were heavy. I felt a weird sensation in my extremities. My heart was beating so fast that I thought it would stop for good. My whole body was under attack, I had trouble breathing, I was suffocating.

Let me out!

Can someone get me out of this chamber of death?

But there was no way out. I was trapped in my body. I had never experienced this intensity before. I screamed for help. Luke woke up and desperately tried to help me. The creaking of a wall or the buzzing of the furnace turned into a piercing hurtful noise. "Make it stop. Make it stop," I kept screaming. Wanting to puncture my ears, I buried my face in my pillow and screamed at the top of my lungs. I was trying to make it stop.

Luke kept saying, "Tell me what to do, tell me what to do."

"I DON'T KNOW. I DON'T KNOW," I cried fearfully.

This terrible suffering is destroying my life. I'm good for nothing. I'm just a big "skinny" pain in the butt for everyone. Luke helped me get out of bed and took me outside; it was three o'clock in the morning. We walked around the block while I cried and cried in desperation. My mind would not stop racing. It was so loud in my head that I wanted to hit my skull on the trees. I kept asking God, "Make it stop, please make it stop." I told Luke for the first time that if the noise and pain don't go away, I want to die, and I meant it. Luke begged me to call my mother. I don't want my mom to know. I don't want her to see me like this. Besides, she can't help. What is she going to do? I don't even understand this torture myself, so how can I explain it to someone else? She is going to think that I'm crazy and send me away.

I don't want to talk about this anymore.

February 7, 2000

This is so crazy, every bit of my anguish is from inside. No one can see my pain. No x-rays can find it. No medical test can tell me what is truly going on. I can't even understand it. Luke sees me crying, but he can't see the emotional wounds, the hurt, the suffering, the pain. It looks like it is up to me to get better, but I just don't know how.

I feel so alone.

Can someone tell me what to do?

I went to see my doctor again and explained what had happened. He immediately changed my medication for a different type of antidepressant and prescribed anti-anxiety pills with it. He said that the anti-anxiety medication would ease the side effects—the additional anxiety and perhaps the crazy attacks. My fears of taking antidepressant are now worse than ever. I'm so afraid of them that I'm thinking of throwing them out.

Should I? Should I try them one more time? My doctor said that it would soon make me feel better.

A journey to self-acceptance – A message of hope, love and courage.

February 10, 2000

That's it. I want to go to the hospital. My nerves are shattered.

NO MORE PAIN. Please, no more pain.

Yesterday, I drove to my regular bank and got lost. I couldn't remember where I was going. I got so scared that I had to pull over. I stopped the car and tried to get myself together. As I sat there, my mind created all kinds of fearful thoughts. I was in trouble. My stomach was cramping. My insides were on fire. I had to go to the bathroom fast. I panicked. There were no public washrooms nearby. I was on a roller coaster, nauseated, burning and cramping. I needed to throw up. It was as if my body wanted to relieve itself of this violent attack. I got back on the road but had no idea if I should be turning right or left. I didn't remember how to get back home. I couldn't believe it. I was lost in my own neighborhood.

Oh, God, I can't even drive anymore. What the heck am I going to do? I can't sleep. I can't eat. I can't take care of my children. I can't be a wife. I can't be a friend. I can't work. I can't laugh. I can't be happy.

SO WHY AM I LIVING?

I'm so freaking skinny that I look like a fragile stick as I walk around the house. The simplest things overwhelm me: cooking, cleaning, taking showers, answering the phone. When I look into my eyes, I see nothing but emptiness. Is there life inside this body? Is there anyone there?

I don't recognize myself. Who am I? WHERE AM I?

I just can't be in this insane world any longer.

No one knows, no one ... I'm so alone.

Can anyone help? Please help me.

February 11, 2000

>Happy tenth birthday, Tyeson.
>I love you, I'm so sorry.
>Mom xoxo

February 20, 2000

I'm having attacks every day. I have them in the morning, in the afternoon, at night, and in between. I can't go anywhere because I'm too afraid to have an episode. Yesterday I had an attack in a grocery store. I had to leave my groceries and rush outside in a panic. My world is becoming so small. I'm feeling even more isolated and lonely.

I'm a prisoner again, this time in my own body.

Where is my power, where is my strength?

Who am I? Who is in charge of my life? What's more, who is in charge of this body? I feel as if I'm living in a nightmare; everything seems blurry and out of proportion. My mind is creating irrational hallucinations; things are moving or jumping around. When I walk up the stairs, I am missing steps because my eyes cannot focus well on distances or heights. Even the floors appear uneven and out of shape. I feel like I'm floating when I'm walking, and I'm constantly nauseated.

Who am I? Where am I? Am I here, in this body?

Right now, my arm seems to be floating away from me. I'm writing yet it feels as if it's happening at a distance. God, what is happening to me? I'm so scared.

Am I crazy?

Today I tried watching television; the voice didn't match the person who was speaking. The picture was moving so quickly I became nauseated and extremely nervous.

I needed to vomit. It was so surreal, and I totally lost it! How small my freaking world is getting? Even reading and writing is bizarrely difficult. Words are moving and jumping randomly on the page. I can't focus. It takes me forever to read and write. I can't adjust my vision or anything in my life. Everything seems twisted and distorted.

Am I possessed?

Sounds drive me crazy, smells make me sick. I'm either too hot or too cold. I'm hypersensitive and constantly anxious. Luke has to use a blender to grind my food because I can't swallow solid food anymore. I'm not comfortable with anyone or anywhere. My whole world is my bedroom. The distortion of my world is unbelievable. I'm afraid that if I see someone they will recognize that I am not here, that somebody or something has taken over my body.

Oh, God, am I haunted by demons?

I feel so small, powerless and scared.

I'm totally lost. Where am I?

February 26, 2000

Yesterday I called Luke at work. I needed help, and he's the only one who knows about my condition, the only one I feel safe with. I've stopped driving for a couple of weeks now and I needed a ride to the hospital. My symptoms were so severe I felt certain I was going to die alone. I have been taking the antidepressants for sometime now and I'm still suffering every minute of the day. Shouldn't they be working by now? Luke drove me to the emergency room and begged me to call my mother again. The doctor checked my heart, and without any compassion suggested bed rest. "You *just* had a panic attack, stop worrying so much," he said. He then prescribed a stronger dose of anti-anxiety pills and left the room. WHY CAN'T ANYONE HELP ME?

What the heck is a panic attack? It sounds like what I have—a panic attack. However, it feels much more than *just* a freaking panic attack. I am suffering in here a whole lot. They just don't understand the torture that I'm going through. How can I explain it? There is no evidence of this freaking pain. The pain no one can understand, it needs to stop. The hospital sent me home without any explanation. I have no understanding of what is happening to me. The doctor at the emergency room squashed all the hope I had left in me of being saved.

If doctors can't help me, who can?

Panic attack … wow! There is a name for one of my symptoms. I had a panic attack, but what about the rest of my suffering? What about the vicious pain, the distortion, my weird vision, the loss of appetite, the diarrhea, the obsessive mind, the anxiety, the nausea, and the insomnia. Please help me to understand. Calm my mind long enough to let me see. Am I stuck in this nightmare forever?

God, don't do this to my children.

I'M SO FREAKING MAD RIGHT NOW.

I'm angry at YOU, at the world, at my life.

I'm asking you for help; WHERE ARE YOU?

I asked for your help years ago to save Jessy; WHERE WERE YOU THEN AND WHERE ARE YOU NOW? I want this suffering to stop, but I don't have the guts to end my life, and I don't have the strength to go on.

IS THERE A GOD OUT THERE?

March 25, 2000

For the past three months, I have been in hell and I'm still living in it. No one should live like this. It truly is hell.

I have been taking my medication for about two months now and nothing, NOTHING is working.

Luke convinced me to call my mother today. It has been weeks since I spoke to her and months since I've seen her. She has no clue what is happening to me.

Can my mother help me?

That is it. I'm going to call her right now.

I am at the end of my rope.

Chapter Six
THE WINDING ROAD TO RECOVERY

I remember my last trip to the emergency room very well. The doctor called my incident *just* a panic attack. I had never heard that term before; although I knew I was anxious and panicky, I had never labeled it. I was unaware such a condition existed. On my way home, I repeated over and over again in my head what the doctor had said, "You *just* had a panic attack." I wondered what he meant by *just* a panic attack. Was he saying that a panic attack was *just* a mild condition, that it was not a big deal? I really did not appreciate the word *just* in his sentence. My condition did not feel like *just* a panic attack; it was a living hell.

When Jessy passed away, I knew why I was in so much pain. This time, however, I could not understand it. I felt there wasn't any reason for me to be suffering in this way, and by the end of March, I was completely housebound, totally agoraphobic. I had no strength to fight anymore; even taking a shower was too much of an effort. It was an ugly world for me out there, and it took all my strength to crawl out of the hole I was in to call my mother. When my mother answered the phone, my heart sank, and I burst into tears. Luke took the phone and tried to explain what was happening. As Luke didn't speak French and my mother spoke only a little English, he just kept repeating, "Something is very wrong with Nancy; she needs help; she needs help." Then Luke gave me back the phone, and somehow, I found the courage to rise above the embarrassment.

I mumbled, "Mom, I think I'm dying." My mother drove all night from Montréal to find me sitting at the dining room table. I couldn't even find the strength to get up and greet her. I just waited for her to come to me. By this time, I was reduced almost to a skeleton. I barely weighed a hundred pounds, the life had been drained out of me as if I had terminal cancer. My mother hardly recognized me, the once strong and healthy daughter she used to know. Instead, she was faced with a daughter who had lost all hope and her way in life.

"Oh, God," she cried. "I'm taking you with me. You need professional help."

Luke tried to explain that doctors had already prescribed different types of medications but nothing seemed to be working.

"Why are they not taking your situation seriously? Do they not see how ill you are? How long have you been this way? Why did you not call me weeks ago?"

Once the shock and interrogation ended, my mother told Luke to pack my things.

"We are leaving right away," she said.

I walked to the car feeling panicky. It had been weeks since I'd been outside. "Mom, I don't think I can do this," I cried.

My intestines wanted to release the "invisible" pain from my body. "Please, God, don't let me embarrass myself in front of my mother," I begged.

Luke helped me to the car, and my mother could not believe the terrible state I was in. With words of encouragement, she opened the door and helped me into the car, gently kissing my forehead. "Everything is going to be fine, Nancy, I am going to help you," she promised.

Letting go of Luke was almost beyond my capability, as for the past year, Luke had been my only safety net. To detach myself from the one and only person I trusted was ripping me apart. The drive to Montréal seemed never-ending. I felt trapped and claustrophobic. My mother tried to keep my mind occupied but my focus was on my symptoms and the brutal separation. I became so uncomfortable that my mother decided to stop at a hotel half way to Montréal. She convinced me to take an anti-anxiety pill.

"You need a break, Nancy. Take one just for tonight."

I had stopped taking the medication weeks ago, as I had read somewhere they were highly addictive. Next morning we arose at 6:00 a.m., leaving right away. I did not want to alarm her but my anxiety was returning. My mother took charge, and I let her. I felt relieved, as if a load of pressure had been lifted off my shoulders. For the first time in a long time, I felt safe with someone besides Luke, and it felt good knowing that my mother truly cared. She was determined to help me. The moment we walked into her house, she sat at the kitchen table and began to figure out ways to get me some help. Seeing how devoted she was, I loved her as I never had before. I had waited thirty-seven years to feel that kind of love and protection from her. Finally, someone was listening to me. My mother had come to save me!

My father's oldest sister was working at a healing center for the soul, and my mother decided to give her a call.

On the phone, a woman name Andrée asked to speak with me. She told me about her five-day intensive program.

Maybe there was hope for me after all.

A journey to self-acceptance – A message of hope, love and courage.

A Return to Source

It was a cold and cloudy spring morning, and I was accompanied by the well-known terror. In the car everyone kept quiet, except, of course, for the voice in my head. I had been making myself sick for over four months; I saw danger everywhere, although none ever existed.

It all began with *one* scary thought, and then that thought created a chain reaction of more scary thoughts. I became trapped in an never-ending cycle of "what if" I am crazy, "what if" I have a serious mental illness, "what if" my husband dies, "what if" my children are in danger ... My heart would start racing, intensifying my senses; my fingers and feet would turn ice cold; and my stomach became upset, cramping and creating dizziness and nausea. The anxiety sent a message to my brain warning my nervous system that something was seriously wrong—"danger is here."

I was having a panic attack.

When we arrived at the healing center, I had another scary thought—the center looked exactly like the convent where I had spent my entire childhood. Tears rolled down my cheeks as I cried to my mother, "Please don't leave me here." Suddenly, I was six years old all over again, and my mother was once again leaving me with strangers.

This old manor building had once been a boarding school and then been made into accommodation for elderly priests and nuns. As we entered the mansion, I froze with fear. What a resemblance! The smell, the walls, the architecture, the nuns, all represented a place of isolation and pain. My mother tried to calm me, but it was too late—I was already travelling down memory lane. We entered the meeting room as two men were welcoming the new arrivals. I did not want to deal with men. I panicked and rushed back to the front lobby. My mother came after me with Andrée, the woman who had spoken to me on the phone. She assured me that no men would approach me unless I wanted them to. For eight days, my mother had been my safety net. She had cared for and protected me like a child. I had come to depend on her and yet somehow I found the courage to hug her and say good-bye. The time had come to get better; it was about recovering and healing. That night Andrée gathered all the newcomers together to discuss all the rules. The rooms we were given were small and without a single window or a picture on the wall, not even a mirror over the sink—and I hated it. Meals were served in the cafeteria, where the nuns prepared the tables and cooked the food. This was déjà-vue. When I entered the self-serve food line, my heart started to race. I panicked and left the room to stand in the hallway with my back against the wall. Andrée tried to help me. "What is happening to you, Nancy? Take a deep breath and talk to me about your fears."

"I feel dizzy and nauseated; I don't think I can eat," I told her. "I'm burning up; intense heat is taking over my body. I'm feeling bewildered and overwhelmed. I think I'm having an attack."

"Tell me more," Andrée said.

"Everything appears out of shape and distorted. Things are moving around me and I seem to be floating. Can you see that? Can you? Am I hallucinating—am I?" I cried.

The depth and severity of my attacks were beyond words. No one could see what I saw and no one could feel what I felt. It was devastating. Andrée grabbed my arm and took me back to the line. "You need to face your fear," she said.

Suddenly I realized that the source of my destructive behavior came from the recollection of my upbringing. A small awakening had begun. I sipped on some orange juice and tried to absorb this new understanding. I had taken the first step towards reclaiming my personal power. I had faced my fear.

Each day from 7:00 a.m. to 10:30 p.m, we sat in the conference room and listened to Andrée speak about the cause and effects of depression. They were long and exhausting days during which I recognized many of my symptoms. I acknowledged the depression within me. I found some comfort in knowing that I was not alone suffering from this devastating condition, and yet I had weird attacks and other bizarre feelings that no one else mentioned, which scared the hell out of me. Every person in the group had been diagnosed with depression. I felt somehow different. I could not fully identify my frightening behavior with anyone else there. *How am I going to recover from it, if no one understands it? Am I the only one suffering from this condition?* I thought to myself.

My aunt Sol-Ange, which means Earth-Angel, worked at the center. I had not seen my aunt for over fifteen years and yet I found myself very comfortable around her. Sol-Ange instantly became a strong influence in my life. This "earth angel" carried me to a place I had never been before. My first experience with meditation was with her. Sol-Ange was employed by Andrée to assist her students in the practice of meditation. Her calming voice was therapeutic to me, and for the first time I became aware of how calming it can be to stop "doing" and to center my intention on one thing only: her voice. During meditation, the noise in my head seemed to want to melt away.

When Sol-Ange stepped into the room, it was as if she had brought the light with her. Her positive energy made me want to be around her always. I learned a lot through her knowledge and experience. She explained that if we really want to be happy and healthy, we must first forgive ourselves. We must let go of all guilt and move on with the flow of life. We must remember where we came from. We must know who we really are. "God created you, Nancy. You are perfect just the way you are. Learn to love yourself. The gifts you will get from it will transform your life. If you want to live your life without fear, stay in the present. Peace comes from within, right here, in this silent moment. Never give up," she said to me.

During meditation, I caught myself wrestling with my fears and frustrations. My thoughts were cluttered and impatient. Yet at some point in the meditation, I gave up my sad story to be in the present moment. However, my mind did not like to stay focused; it jumped back and forth, in and out of the past and the future constantly. Nonetheless, I now had a glimpse of what a break from my terrors felt like. In the end, Sol-Ange taught me how to dream again. Although she did not experience my symptoms, she understood emotional pain. She provided enough insights and gave me wisdom that would later come to rescue me. Through her care, I regained some of my life back and found the willpower to go on and the determination to get better. My aunt's healing power had opened the gate to a new path, a different way to live my life. I could see a spiritual road ahead, one I could choose for myself.

I have only grateful memories of Andrée. Her mother suffered for years from chronic anxiety and panic attacks, and, determined to help her and others, Andrée embarked on a journey of study to understand the cause and effect of people's behavior. She had opened her heart and started a course for people willing and ready to heal themselves. Her healing process (the work) begins with acknowledging, listening, and comforting the little child that resides within us. She believes that the recognition of the little child in us is the beginning of self-healing. I found her healing techniques very powerful. They helped me to recognize where my pain was coming from, as we did hours of writing and soul searching and then spent time on sharing, surrendering, and meditating. We also talked about God and the power of love. We really learned how to embrace our true selves. It was during one of my severe panic attacks that Andrée shared some of her mother's story with me. I finally heard about someone whose experience was similar to my own. Listening to Andrée made a big difference; it eased the pressure of not knowing what was happening to me. Andrée had been successful in assisting her mother in recovering, and she believed that she could do the same thing for me. That night, a light dawned and I felt as if a window of hope had opened. When you bring hope into a dark moment, the energy instantly shifts away from desperation. "Hope is the restoration of the appetite for life itself," Wayne Dyer says in his wonderful book, *There's a Spiritual Solution to Every Problem*. It is the return to seeing life optimistically. Hope gives us the energy to get through obstacles. I now had the appetite to change, to get better, and to live again.

At the end of each afternoon, we were asked to write about difficult events in our past and upbringing. Andrée wanted us to search deep within ourselves to arrive at the root of our suffering. She wanted us to feel the pain and to write about it. So we spent hours reflecting on our lives and trying to be true to ourselves. At our last group meeting, Andrée asked us to bring our letters with us to the assembly. I was surprised and shocked when she asked us to read them in front of everyone. In fact, I freaked out, as I had written things I had never told anyone; now I had to share my deepest secrets with the entire group. I had written about my deep sadness, my anger, the convent, Jessy's death, my absent father, and also about my years of dancing in bars. I wanted to run away and hide.

As we sat in a circle, my turn to share was quick to arrive. It took everything I had to read what I had written. I was shaking and crying, and I almost had to stop reading. Surprisingly, I received compassion, love, and positive feedback from the group. It felt good to let it all out, and as I told my story, something amazing happened. I felt lighter. I felt freer; it was not so serious anymore. It was simply a story. I knew it would never hurt that badly again. Shortly after, we were asked to go for a walk, and we found ourselves standing in front of a huge metal garbage bin at the back of the mansion. Inside the bin a fire was burning and everyone stood there in silence when Andrée said, "It's time to let go and let God." Wow! I had never heard a more powerful sentence. Suddenly, we all knew what to do—every word we had written went up in flames. It was so uplifting, and it was healing. Andrée's words kept singing in my head: "It's time to let go and let God. It's time to let go and let God." It was this statement that started me thinking about God again.

One afternoon when I went back to my room I saw that someone had placed a rocking chair in the corner. I then heard a knock on the door. When I opened the door, I was face to face with a man named Robert. Robert would show up from time to time to give us support. I had seen him many times before, yet had never known him. Robert asked if he could enter my room. Nervously, I let him in. He sat in the rocking chair, and gently asking me to join him. "Come here and let me cradle you," he said. I stood in front of him with my heart palpitating. "I know how much you miss your dad. Come and let me comfort you," he offered. Andrée must have told him about my letters. I felt embarrassed, yet I suddenly found myself wanting this man's affection, as he spoke like a caring father. "I'm not here to hurt you. I'm here to love and comfort you. Let me be here for you," he said. To my surprise, I moved toward him and sat on his knee. I put my head on his shoulder, allowing myself to let go like a little child. I cried for my father, and a lifelong sorrow lifted from my heart. This man had reached into my soul. I closed my eyes and felt my father's love. When I couldn't cry anymore, I looked up and simply said, "Thank you." We sat silently together for a while as I embraced the moment. That same year I reconciled with my dad at last. I had learned to accept and love him for the man that he is. Today I have a loving and healthy relationship with my father. Healing had truly taken place on that amazing afternoon with Robert.

A journey to self-acceptance – A message of hope, love and courage.

When it was time for me to go back to my mother's home, I felt that I was not entirely ready to do so. I had started to understand some of my behavior but I needed more time to process it. I now had the tools and skills to cope with my condition and I expected to see a transformation, or at least some kind of pain relief. However, this did not happen. I was not one whose life miraculously changed overnight. I had to get my health back little by little, and I really do mean little by little. I faced days of frustration, weeks of depression, and months in constant anxiety. For two more years I lived my life with this overwhelming condition. Unfortunately, I was still focusing on my symptoms and obsessing about what was wrong with me. I was stuck on the negative feelings. If I had taken the time to sit quietly and count the good things in my life, even if they felt extremely few at the time, the good would have eventually grown and I would have felt much better sooner. Counting our blessings when we are in pain takes great effort and devotion, especially when we are experiencing a very dark phase in our lives. However, this will teach us into thinking differently, developing the healthy habit of being grateful rather than being fearful, angry, or resentful. I had a lot to learn and understand. My newfound information had not yet entered my heart. I was still living in my head. However, even though I couldn't feel it for months, my health was slowly improving, as I was willing to change and see life differently.

During the stay at the healing center, Andrée and Sol-Ange had planted the seed of hope within me. One thing I had learned was never give up, so I continued on my road to recovery one step at a time. I held tightly onto my hopes and dreams, even during the toughest times. I understood that now it was really up to me to help myself.

Slowly, I began to realize how precious my life was and truly is.

God always sends angels to watch over us.
—Anonymous

A meeting with Andrée, in my own words:
Perfectionism is a mask to cover the fear of not being good enough. I sat and reflected on these words of wisdom from Andrée.

Choosing the spiritual path doesn't mean that you will always have a smooth or easy road to walk; however, you will always be aligning with the higher power.

Firstly, stop obsessing about what other people think of you. Concentrate on your own Truth and see how liberating it can be.

It takes courage and honesty to move from your head to your heart. Living with an open heart is living authentically, and it is always worthwhile.

Loving yourself means learning to let go of a lifetime of negative messages.

You cannot change the past, but you do have the power to alter how you think about it—changing how you see the past will change the moment, and therefore your future. The present is a gift; find it, stay with it, and it will change your life.

Understand that every thought provokes its own chemistry.
I had not known that before.

A journey to self-acceptance – A message of hope, love and courage.

Everything you think, say, and do comes from either fear or love. Awareness is the key to a harmonious life and happiness—face your fears and as you journey through them, don't look back—love is *here* waiting for you.

If you can think yourself into an anxiety attack, then you can think yourself out of it.

Awareness is the first step in moving towards self-transformation, and the *will* to change is the next step to healing.
I understand that, but please, can someone tell me how to do it?

Don't let your mind and outer circumstances control your life.

True power is within … heart and soul … it's in every breath you take.
Okay, but how can I get out of my mind? It's so overpowering.

It takes time, training, devotion and faith in God.
But I want to feel better now. How long is this going to take?

Once you've had enough, you consider the possibility that there might be another way, a better way. I took a long look at myself and recognized the unhealthy ways I was thinking, and so I tried hard to break this harmful habit. What a challenge it was! Understanding my behavior was one thing, changing it was another. It seemed that my mind had a mind of its own. It kept slipping back to its old habits of worrying and anticipating all sorts of things. Still, I faced the next chapter of my life with determination. I did not give up, even though I did not receive a miracle. I had gained courage, and I worked hard on training my mind, hopeful that one day I would rise above it.

When I left the healing center, my mother had arranged a mini vacation for us, at which time I felt deep love for her. Instead of the old resentful feelings, I felt content in her company, and this is when I began to notice the changes in myself. I felt the power of love in a way that I had not known existed. I started to eat a little more and gained a few pounds, which made me look healthier, and I was becoming stronger. Every day I had a therapeutic massage, and my anxiety decreased during each session. I felt less anxious because my mind focused on the masseuse's hands and not on my symptoms. My attention was on feeling good. For a moment, I let go of my sad story, and I found myself in the present moment where it was peaceful and good.

One afternoon on the way back to the hotel, my mother decided to stop at a mall, and she wanted me to join her. This was a major step; I viewed all malls with fear, as if they were overbearing monsters without any exit for escape. My mother did not allow my anxiety to stop me; she grabbed my arm and forced me in. "Remember to face your fear, Nancy," she said. Walking through the mall, I felt as if I were back on a roller coaster. I became dizzy and nauseated. After twenty minutes, I couldn't stand it anymore so I sat down on a bench and waited for my mother to finish her shopping. From where I was sitting, I could see four incredible words on the cover of a book in a store window: *From Panic to Power*. I walked in, picked up the book, and was amazed at its content. I asked the sales person if the book had been translated into French; it hadn't. I had never read an English book before, and so I put it back on the shelf. However, on my way out of the mall, I was overwhelmed with the feeling to return and purchase the book, and so I went back *without my mother* and bought it. This was my second step toward healing. That night, I read for hours. I was reading my own story. Lucinda was my story, and she had recovered!

Oh, sweet heaven, was this book written just for me? The road to recovery did not seem so dark and narrow or impossible anymore.

It was a new beginning.

My way home

It had been four weeks since I had seen my family, and again I had to face being a mother. I also realized I had no desire to do so, or even to go home. The thought of returning troubled me a great deal. This is hard to say, but I didn't even want to see my children. The overbearing feeling of duty made me constantly on edge. I felt burdened with responsibility. I found myself drowning once more in a panic attack. I ran outside, desperately looking for air to lessen the burning sensation I was experiencing inside. My stepfather, who was sitting at the dining room table, saw me struggling to breathe and came to rescue me. He wrapped me in his powerful arms and whispered, "It's okay, Nancy. Everything is going to be fine. You don't have to be afraid, because your family loves you. Just let go and let God take care of you."

Wow! God again. I had forgotten about *Him*.

My stepfather's tender words helped me back into a safe place. During these difficult times, I needed to be reminded of God, and Léo had brought God back into my world at the perfect moment. By hearing God's name, I was released from my fears.

As I am writing these words today, tears are rolling down my face. My wonderful stepfather Léo died last year at the age of sixty-two. His death was unexpected and shocking. He had been a strong, active, and healthy father, grandfather, and stepfather. Léo, you made such an impact on our lives—an outstanding husband for my mother, an extraordinary grandfather for all the children, you touched our hearts in a way that no other father figure ever had. I will never forget that night when you rushed to rescue me. Your strong arms and kind, compassionate words will remain in my heart forever. You are truly my hero. I love you, and I miss you so very much.

Next morning, I faced the day with a little more strength. I stood at the window waiting apprehensively for my family to arrive. They had left Toronto at sunrise and we expected them to arrive before noon. My eyes filled with tears and I became very emotional as I saw my children getting out of the van. Although I was extremely nervous, I felt a great joy in my heart. There they were, my wonderful children, with pretty flowers in their tiny hands, smiling happily, yet nervously. Their faces, oh, my God, their beautiful faces—I missed them so very much. I hugged and kissed them, and I loved them with all my heart. When I turned around and saw my husband, also with flowers, I rushed to throw myself into his arms as his eyes filled with tears. I could not believe how much I had missed him. He looked as worried and concerned as my children, yet I could feel his happiness. I had finally found shelter in my husband's arms. We stayed that night at my mother's house, talking and holding each other. We spoke all evening about the four weeks that had just passed. Luke's devotion and love helped to ease my pain. There was no need for anything else; being together was enough.

My stepfather and mother took their responsibility as grandparents seriously. We could hear our children laughing through the walls. It brought joy and comfort to my heart, and I promised myself that I would get well very soon. Next morning, we were on the road home. I tried to hide my anxiety, although I had to ask Luke to turn off the radio because I was still struggling with hypersensitivity. Sounds and smells created an enormous amount of anxiety in me, greatly affecting my state of mind. I did not want to alarm him but I needed to be honest and so I had to tell him the truth, the absolute truth. He needed to know how severe my condition was so he would be able to help with my recovery. The seven-hour drive home was extremely uncomfortable for me. I tried to read, but crazy thoughts persistently troubled me. I was anticipating the housework, preparing dinners, laundry, cleaning, homework, and looking after my children. It was too much for me. *Oh, God,* I thought, *how am I going to do it all, when I can't even take care of myself?* When I arrived home, I ran to my bedroom and collapsed. I was too weighed down to see the harmful direction I was taking. I needed to trust that there is a power in the universe greater than I. Unable to escape from the torments of my mind, I sank into a dark hole once again and suffered terribly.

They say knowledge is power—but only if we use it.

Realizing that I could not free myself from my condition overnight drove me to despair. Luke held me in his arms and said to me, "I am here for you; together we can get through this. Tell me what you need and I will do everything I can to get it for you." That night, I let him into my frightening world. I gave him the book *From Panic to Power*, by Lucinda Bassett. We sat on the bed and read it together. "My God, Nancy, it must be like being on a bad trip from using drugs," he said.

But this nightmare would not end. Luke took over the household chores, groceries, laundry, vacuuming, and cleaning. In the evenings, he would take the children to their soccer and baseball games and make sure they showered before bed. Week after week, he did everything. My family doctor recommended I see a psychologist right away. I found this very embarrassing, because I believed that people who saw psychologists were seriously damaged or maybe even crazy. *Perhaps I'm all that!* I thought to myself.

On my first visit, the psychologist asked me about my breathing. "You are hyperventilating. Your breathing is too fast; breathe slower," she said. She documented my breathing habits and yet did nothing about it, apart from telling me to breathe slower. Nevertheless, the term "hyperventilation" resonated with me.

The following month, I went to the library with a friend, and, I realized the word "hyperventilating" was still on my mind, I picked up a book called *Hyper-Ventilation Syndrome*, by Dinah Bradley. I read it in two days. I could not believe what I was reading. All my symptoms were in the book: chronic anxiety, palpitations, headaches, lack of concentration, breathlessness, upset stomach, sex problems, chest pains, frequent yawning, nightmares, low self-confidence, panic attacks, exhaustion, low energy, mental fuzziness, tingling sensations, dizziness, nausea, irritable bowel syndrome, and feeling spaced out. I had it all!

This little book explained it extremely well. It explained why hyperventilating is an incorrect way to breathe and can lead to chronic health problems.

> *Hyperventilation means using the lungs to move more air in and out of the chest than the body can deal with.*
> — Dinah Bradley
> *Hyper-Ventilation Syndrome*

The solution to this condition is determination, training, and understanding.

I can do that! I thought.

I couldn't believe it; I had to learn how to breathe again. I read the book once more, doing all the exercises suggested. I worked hard on retraining my breathing patterns daily. I timed my breath, knowing that I should be breathing around twelve to fourteen breaths per minute instead of twenty to twenty-two. I also learned that chest breathing causes the diaphragm to lose its flexibility and strength. Like any other group of muscles that is not exercised, the diaphragm needs training to gain its strength and flexibility before it can be used to its full capacity. During my daily breathing exercises, I placed a book on my stomach just below my navel and watched my tummy rise as I inhaled and fall as I exhaled. Relearning to use my diaphragm instead of my upper chest muscles took time and effort. I had to learn to regulate my breathing, breathe in for two to three seconds, and breathe out for three to four seconds. This was challenging and felt unnatural, and yet with time, I found it relaxing.

Luke's mother came to help during weekdays, as my healing was a slow process. I spent most of my time in my bedroom reading about my condition. I read everything I could find on anxiety, panic disorder, agoraphobia, and depression. I was searching for answers, hoping to find solutions. When my anxiety wasn't quite as severe, I somehow found the strength to go downstairs, finding comfort in my favorite chair to watch my children play, though my anxiety would quickly turn to panic, making me retreat back to my room.

During this time, a good friend of mine, Manon, who had moved to Australia, learned about my condition and she called me. It had been a long time since we had spoken. The moment she asked me how I was feeling, I burst into tears. I told her my sad story and she immediately offered to help. Manon had planned to return to visit her family and she told me she would extend her trip and spend the rest of the summer with me. It felt as if someone had answered my prayers. It was the right person at the right time offering their help. Manon helped with the cooking and house cleaning. She also drove me to workshops, to therapy, to books stores, and anywhere else I needed to go. She also taught me about nutrition. This was when my journey to healthy living really started. We would go to the library on a weekly basis and borrow videos on health and nutrition. It surprised me to see how fascinated and interested I became about health. I began to buy self-help books and spent hours reading about the importance of food and exercise on the human body. I quickly learned that a poor diet and lack of exercise effects not only the body, but the mind as well. It affects the way the brain works.

At the end of the summer, Manon had to leave and I was heartbroken. Having Manon around had forced me out of the bedroom to socialize more. Her friendship meant a great deal to me; however, now I had a little more strength to deal with my anxiety. I was able to cook healthy dinners and take care of some of the household chores. The children started the school year, and I used this time to read the piles of books I had bought that summer. The more a learned about my condition, the less it frightened me. At the end of August, I decided to see the new psychiatrist that my doctor recommended. There were no windows in the small room and it made me feel claustrophobic. I asked if I could leave the door open and her response shocked me; she flatly refused. She simply said no. *What kind of shrink is she?* I thought to myself. My thoughts were wild with judgment. *Who does she think she is? Isn't she supposed to make her patient feel a little better or at least more comfortable?* I found her to be very insensitive and unfriendly. She sat in her doctor's chair and waited for me to speak.

"Why are you here?" she asked.

"I need help," I replied.

Then, silence again. She waited for me to speak. I expected a question of some type or expert advice from her, but I got nothing. She sat there in silence. I received the same silent treatment the following week. I could not wait to get out of her office, and yet, I went back.

The next visit, I asked her, "Why don't you ask me any questions? I feel so uncomfortable sitting in this confined room without speaking."

"I'm waiting for you to open up," she answered. Then she asked again, "Why are you here?"

Wow! I need to say something or this will go on forever, I thought.

She sat only a few feet away and her constant staring bothered me. During the silence, I was struggling with my breathing. One minute, I was hyperventilating and the next, I was holding my breath. I tried again and again to tell her my story, but with every attempt, my stomach did somersaults.

Initially, I went to her sessions because it gave me something to do during the week. My children were back at school and since Manon had left for Australia, I felt lonely and I was not ready to deal with the outside world.

On my fourth visit, I decided to face my fears and I spilled my guts out. I spoke of my deep anguish and told her exactly how sick and depressed I had been for the past year. She stopped me, but only because my time was up. I was angry; she did not say a word, she didn't answer any of my questions, and she did not share her expertise with me. She just sat there and stared. I don't even know if she heard me. Was she listening? *What kind of profession is this? You need a university degree for this! Anyone can do it!* I thought in anger. Yet, I found myself sitting in her office again and again. I kept talking and she kept silent. I spoke and she listened. However, as I was speaking one day, I finally heard my thinking, I heard what I was saying—an awareness was coming, and it hit me like a ton of bricks. I recognized what I had been doing to myself, and then an amazing thing happened—I started to answer my own questions. After many weeks of complaining and feeling sorry for myself, I suddenly became sick and tired of hearing my sad story. I was finally willing and ready to move on. I was tired of being locked away from the outside world. I faced the agoraphobia and signed up for my first yoga class.

I wondered if the therapist's silent treatment was part of her strategy. Did she keep quiet to allow me to understand my behavior so that I could take control of my life? I think she knew exactly what she was doing. Her silence challenged me to listen and do the inner work; it permitted me to see and feel for myself. As our work continued, she started to ask questions and send me home with assignments. "Reflect on this and come back with an open heart," she said. She knew how to approach every situation. We investigated my fears one at a time and looked deeply into the root of my anguish with compassion and understanding. Every week I had a new challenge to face. In a few months, the chronic anxiety finally began to decrease. I saw my therapist with a new attitude, in a new light. After nearly six months, I knew I did not need weekly sessions. However, I looked forward to our monthly sessions. She gave me information to read and things to write about. She was a strong influence in my life. We worked together for two years, until we both knew the therapy was no longer needed. She asked me to give up my place for someone who really needed it. I was okay with it, as I was ready.

I remember my therapist's last words. "In my practice, I see two types of people. There are those who expect me to heal them and do the work for them. They blame the world, their parents, their husband, and their past for their unhappiness. They are not ready or willing to see, to meet their thoughts with understanding, and to be fully responsible for their lives. Then there are those who are confused by the pain, but truly want to see. They are willing to do the work to get better. They have the drive, discipline, and willpower to change. They are open to be a hundred percent responsible for their own health and happiness. These people come to me for assistance, not knowing that they have the answers within themselves. These people leave knowing that they are in charge of their lives. They know that I am only here to guide them on their journey, not to heal them. Nancy, you are one of these people.

"Remember, no matter which road you take, you cannot fail to arrive home."

A journey to self-acceptance – A message of hope, love and courage.

Our last conversation made me realize how strong and ready I was. I was willing to change and knew I had the power to do so.

Yes, I am that person she described. I am all that! I said to myself.

Today's reflection

> *Impatience is only another form of resistance. It is resistance to learning and to changing. When we demand that it be done right now, completed at once, then we don't give ourselves time to learn the lesson involved with the problem we have created.*
>
> —Louise L. Hay
> *You Can Heal Your Life*

The call to my spiritual journey took place in 1999. At the age of thirty-six, I was forced to look at myself and stop the soul-killing things I was doing, but my mind overshadowed my heart. I was not yet ready.

At the age of thirty-seven, things had to get really bad before a change could take place. I truly needed to hit rock bottom before I recognized that I had to do something about it. Halfway to recovery, I hit rock bottom again. The problem was that I wanted overnight to become an ideal human being who found everlasting happiness. I wanted to see results immediately. First, I had to face the sorrow that stood in front of me. In fact, I could not regain my health until I dealt with the part of me that was resisting and hurting. The process needed all my courage, time, compassion, honesty, and silence, but I did not like the step-by-step process towards my recovery. I was impatient. I was resisting the lessons I had to learn. I did not fully understand the link between my thoughts and feelings. I did not realize something greater than my mind existed, and for true healing to take place, I had to *stop* and *feel*. I had to be willing to change and see life differently. I had to start remembering an essential part of myself, my heart.

At the age of thirty-eight, a battle started between the person I used to be and the person I wanted to become. The old me, out of habit, kept coming back to sabotage my progress. I quickly realized I had to be incredibly vigilant and disciplined to put the old me to rest.

Then, suddenly, one day I started to question everything. I questioned my relationship with God, my life and myself.

Who am I? I wondered.
Where did I come from?
Is there a God out there?
What is the purpose of my life?
Why don't I feel excited about anything? Why can't I be truly happy? Why?

During this time, I had been diagnosed with panic and obsessive-compulsive thinking disorder. I was also diagnosed with generalized anxiety disorder and depression. I did not get caught up in my psychiatrist's analysis. It only gave me a starting place, a chance to educate myself about these conditions.

At thirty-nine, my soul screamed ENOUGH—I'd had enough! I came to a point where I could not live with my personal story any longer. I'd had enough of being tormented and unhappy. I knew in my very being that I had to create my self anew. I also had to remember my true self. I came into this world *whole*, with no worries, no fears, no beliefs, no baggage. I was born with a clear mind, content and happy. Yet on my way through life, I lost myself. I left my true self behind and took on a false identity. I had forgotten where I came from. The day I remembered who I truly am would be the day I would be free. I knew in my heart this day was coming. In addition to the strong desire to become *present* in my life, I had to let go of so many unhealthy aspects of my personality that I had developed over the years: worrying, anticipating, perfectionism, attachments, and high expectations, all connected to past memories, shame and based-fear.

The first year of my healing was challenging indeed. I struggled daily with my obsessive mind. I refused to accept my pain or my life as it was, resisting and fighting continually, unaware of my actions most of the time. However, I slowly began to understand I am here to evolve, to learn particular lessons to advance me in my spiritual journey. The recognition of my faulty breathing pattern was to be the first of my step-by-step process. But it needed awareness and presence; being aware was not a simple task. It did not enter my world easily. Then, one day, for a brief moment, I discovered *stillness*. I found a true moment of serenity. This happened during Shivasana in yoga. I understood at a deeper level the concept and power of living in the *now*. It took me to a place I had never been before. Finally, *deliverance*!

All my life, I had taken my breathing for granted, never thinking about it. I didn't ask myself if I was breathing correctly. I just assumed I was. Breathing happens without effort, without consent. It simply happens on its own. We never think about it, we just do it. That day, I found myself breathing consciously, and from the act of being present, I discovered a place in my mind to rest. This wonderful place was in the space I created between my thoughts. I cannot express enough how important our breathing is. The practice of *conscious breathing* slows down brain activity and takes us to a place of stillness where we communicate not in the language of words, but of feelings. This powerful practice calms the nervous system, quiets the mind, and brings a sense of calmness and serenity from the inside out. Conscious breathing is awareness of the breath in our bodies. The breath is the link between the mind, body, and spirit. It is a channel to the answers within us—the outlet to connect us to our higher self.

Harmony can be found in quiet moments when we come together with the divinity in us. When we breathe mindfully, we find peace in the space we have created between our thoughts—we know who we really are, and that we are never alone, as God lives within us. We know he speaks to us every minute of every hour of every day.

The practice of conscious breathing has transformed my neurotic personality to a more peaceful one. It has brought me presence and moments of freedom. Unfortunately, no one ever talks about the importance of the breath, not even educated practitioners. Nevertheless, I am going to talk about it. I want the whole world to know how vital the practice of conscious breathing truly is. The calmness I felt during Shivasana in yoga took me out of the insane world I had created. My mind stopped and the awareness stayed with me long enough that I could feel the harmony between my mind, body, and spirit. At that moment, I had created space within for absolute freedom. For a brief instant, I recognized my true self—not my physical body, but the being within, my soul. I experienced what I call today *True Liberation*. Since that time, I've cherished that moment in my heart—never forgetting the feeling of unity and peace that I experienced through profound stillness.

In a few months, I realized that practicing conscious breathing every day was essential for my well-being and sanity, and so I embarked on a new path. I opened myself up to the art of meditation and mindfulness yoga. I wanted to train my mind to slow down, to be in the now. Within a few months, I noticed that the more I breathed consciously, the broader the space between my thoughts became. I found myself resting peacefully longer and longer within the gaps. As a result, I discovered tranquility and felt relief. Finally, my mind slowed down; it was not so neurotic anymore. I was now supported by a new sensation, Inner Calmness.

The practice of conscious breathing was challenging indeed; it needed patience and determination. Nevertheless, it was and still is the greatest blessing of my life.

> One day,
> my soul screamed,
> true power is within!
> Where there is space,
> there is peace.
> Where there is silence,
> there is harmony.
> In the gap,
> I rest.
> In the breath,
> I am.
> Consciously breathing,
> I will be,
> divine energy.

There are some people who say that diagnosing a condition is not always a good thing. It may keep us trapped in the situation. My experience says otherwise. Knowing about my condition gave me the chance to educate myself, to understand my behavior and to improve my life. It allowed me to move forward. Recently a word came to my attention—depersonalization. I decided to Google the word.

"Depersonalization disorder is a dissociative disorder in

which the sufferer is affected by persistent or recurrent feelings of depersonalization and/or derealization. Diagnostic criteria include persistent or recurrent experiences of feeling detached from one's mental processes or body," I read.

The core symptom of depersonalization disorder is the subjective experience of unreality, and as such, there are no clinical signs. Common descriptions are: watching oneself from a distance; out-of-body experience; a sense of just going through the motions; feeling as one is in a dream or movie; not feeling in control of one's speech or physical movements; and feeling detached from one's own thoughts or emotions. Individuals with the disorder commonly describe a feeling as though time is "passing" by them and they are not in the notion of the present. Theses experiences may cause a person to feel uneasy or anxious since they strike at the core of a person's identity and consciousness.

Fear of going crazy, brain damage, and losing control are common complaints.

—From Wikipedia, the free encyclopaedia
www.wikipedia.org/wiki/Depersonalisation_disorder

This information made me understand what happened during my severe panic attacks and acute stress.

Chapter Seven
YOGA

Yoga is like my spine; without it, I would surely collapse.
—A student of yoga

A Moment of Truth

Yesterday is gone.
No anticipations, fears, or worries—
trust in absolute silence,
deliverance can be found!
The Lord says, *Find your feet.*
I am in your steps.
For as this instant, you are free.

As a teenager, I read to escape reality. Whenever I felt sad or lonely, I lost myself in a fictional love story. Yet I spent most of my twenties without reading a single book. I suppose I was too busy working and shopping. In my mid thirties, I again found the desire to read. This time it was not to escape my feelings, but to educate myself. I wanted to learn and transform my life, deep down; I wanted to remember *who I am.*

I searched for the answers; it did not matter what type of spiritual books I read or which video tapes I watched or what kind of workshops

I attended, they always recommended yoga and meditation. My first experience with meditation was with my aunt Sol-Ange at the healing mansion. When I returned from my mother's home, I tried to meditate on my own but felt uncomfortable sitting alone. I didn't understand the work, the discipline, or the time consumed for this spiritual practice. Soon afterwards, I gave it up. Several months later, I mentioned to a friend my desire to try yoga. I had no idea where to find a good yoga studio. Frankly, I had little incentive and no self-confidence. My friend giggled, "Nancy, there is a yoga studio right in front of my apartment. I can see it from my window. It's called Helen Duquette Yoga Studio."

"Wow, a French teacher!" I assumed she was French because of her last name. "This must be a sign. This has to be the one," I said.

By this time, I had been working with my therapist for about three months and I have just begun to feel as though it could be working. I felt more courageous and wanted to take this opportunity to challenge myself. I was strong enough to face the agoraphobia and so I decided to step into the unknown. My world had to expand; seeing my therapist once a week was not enough. Yoga was a new step, a new adventure, a new place—all of a sudden, my mind went wild: *It's probably in a confined place, with shut doors, and overcrowded, and without an exit ...* I panicked! Before going for my first lesson, I called the teacher. I wanted to make sure that I was welcome. Calling her turned out to be a smart move. Her kindness and understanding put me at ease. She suggested I take a place by the door just in case I needed to leave quickly. Looking back, I realize I had taken another step toward my recovery. I had opened up my world to a complete stranger. The following morning, I prepared for my first yoga class and found myself on the road to self-exploration. Not sure what to expect, I stayed beside the wall next to the door. Everyone was on the ground resting in a pose called Shivasana, their eyes closed, and they seemed to be sleeping. When the class started, I was tense, while the rest of the class seemed to move elegantly with great flexibility. Each student was attentive and worked gracefully on every pose the instructor was teaching, while I was rigid and agitated. After an hour and a half of yoga, which seemed more like three hours to me, we laid down again on the mat for Shivasana, and I thought to myself, *I didn't feel anything. I'm not feeling any better. I'm still anxious.*

"Nancy, you came here with a closed heart, with an attitude, hesitant and full of judgment. You are impatient; open your heart and your mind will open up to receive." My heart said.

My mind was shallow. I believed yoga was no more than a stretching exercise. Yet everywhere I turned for help, there it was—yoga for the mind, yoga for the heart, yoga for the soul, yoga for well-being …

> *Spiritual practices that involve the physical body, such as t'ai chi, qigong, and yoga, are also increasingly being embraced in the Western world. These practices do not create a separation between body and spirit and are helpful in weakening the pain-body. They will play an important role in the global awakening.*
>
> —Eckhart Tolle
> *A New Earth*

I had experienced yoga for an hour and a half and had already decided I did not like it. I was bored with the physical exercises and received no mental or spiritual satisfaction. Nevertheless, going to yoga helped me to get out of the house and forced me to socialize.

What is it about yoga? I don't get it, I asked myself every week. Although I did not get it, I wanted to understand it very much. Six months passed and my thoughts on yoga still hadn't changed. Nonetheless, I stuck with it. I kept going to my classes and did whatever the teacher asked—downward dog, cat pose, warrior poses, balance poses, etc. My mind had not yet connected with my body and soul. It was stubborn. The instructor used words like *awareness* and *consciousness*, but these words were not in my vocabulary. I did not understand their meaning. During yoga, I looked around, judging and analyzing everyone and everything. I compared my postures with others to see if I was more flexible. I was in a competitive state of mind. I did not know how to be present, how to be attentive, or how to look inside myself. I was too busy commenting on everything, criticizing, and trying to make myself look good. My full attention was on the outside. I had no connection with my inner-self, and so I wondered why yoga did not work—but it was working. It is always working, but it happens slowly. I just couldn't see it. I was lost in my ego, not knowing that something greater within the physical body exists.

The expression *mindfulness* was often used during yoga, but again the word meant nothing to me. Shivasana, the pose that we do at the beginning and end of each class, began to arouse my curiosity. The teacher kept saying how important this pose is, and yet we were doing nothing. We lay down, waited for the teacher to speak, and a few minutes later, the class began. In fact, the class had already begun; it had started with Shivasana, I just wasn't aware of it. My mind could not stop chattering, although during Shivasana, I did catch myself hearing a word or two from my teacher. She talked about quieting the mind or something like that.

For thirty-seven years, my mind has never stopped, not even for a second. *How can we quiet a mind?* I wondered. Her words seemed like a foreign language to me. I went home puzzled. *How can anyone empty their mind and find freedom in their body? How can I clear my mind and make it empty? Is this possible? Is this what Shivasana is? Can anyone do this?*

Shivasana, I kept repeating in my head. Everyone seemed to love it and looked so peaceful in it. Maybe, someday, somehow, something would happen to me during my time in Shivasana.

Week after week, I turned to Helen Duquette's yoga studio and my therapist to get me out of the house and face my fears. The rest of my free time, I read. Through my reading, I began to understand the relationship I could have between my higher self and yoga. First, the idea of a *soul* within was difficult for me to grasp because I lived in the concept that I was mainly a physical body. However, the words I read in my spiritual books started to connect me to my yoga practice.

> *Read everything you can to expand your awareness and understanding of how the mind works. There is so much knowledge out there for you. This book is only ONE STEP on your pathway! Get other viewpoints. Hear other people say it in a different way. Study with a group for a while until you go beyond them.*
> *This is a life work. The more you learn, the more you know, the more you practice and apply, the better you get to feel, and the more wonderful your life will be. Doing this work makes YOU FEEL GOOD!*
> —Louise L. Hay
> *You Can Heal Your Life*

A journey to self-acceptance – A message of hope, love and courage.

Bhagavad-Gita
A New Translation by Stephen Mitchell

The mind is restless, unsteady,
turbulent, wild, stubborn;
truly, it seems to me
as hard to master as the wind.

The blessed Lord said:

You are right, Arjuna: the mind
is restless and hard to master;
but by constant practice and detachment,
it can be mastered in the end.

Yoga is indeed hard
for those who lack self-restraint;
but if you keep striving earnestly,
in the right way, you can reach it. (6.33-36) page 95

When his mind becomes clear and peaceful,
he enters absolute joy;
his passions are calmed forever;
he is utterly absorbed in God. (6.19-23) page 93

Constantly mastering his mind,
the man of yoga grows peaceful,
attains supreme liberation,
and vanishes into my bliss. (6.14-18) page 91

Nothing in the world can purify
as powerfully as wisdom;

practiced in yoga, you will find
this wisdom within yourself. (4.37-41) page 79

Mature in yoga, impartial
everywhere that he looks,
he sees himself in all beings
and all beings in himself.

The man who sees me in everything
and everything within me
will not be lost to me, nor
will I ever be lost to him.

He who is rooted in oneness
realizes that I am
in every being; wherever
he goes, he remains in me.

When he sees all beings as equal
in suffering or in joy
because they are like himself,
that man has grown perfect in yoga. (6.29-32) page 94

When the mind constantly runs
after the wandering senses,
it drives away wisdom, like the wind
blowing a ship off course. 2.67-71) page 59

The undisciplined have no wisdom,
no one-pointed concentration;
with no concentration, no peace;
with no peace, where can joy be? (2.62-66) page 58

The word *yoga* comes from the Sanskrit language and means to unite or to harmonize. With time, I discovered that yoga is more than a system of physical exercises; it is a spiritual pathway to harmonize body, mind, and spirit, coming together with the higher self. Whatever the reason, yoga brings its countless benefits to all who practice it.

My determination to find the freeing feeling of yoga made me sign up for a second class at the recreation center. I also went on my first yoga retreat, and I looked forward to the eleven hours of yoga as well as the free time to read and walk the grounds in nature. I was also hoping for a change in my yoga; however, the long hours of yoga were rather overwhelming. Still, I survived it gracefully.

In the summer of 2002, I took a break from yoga and spent the entire summer with my children. It was nice not to think about yoga or the reason I did not get it! The entire two months, I went rollerblading, took nature walks, and played tennis with my children. My energy level had increased and the sun helped my state of mind. I was not fully aware of the changes that had taken place in my body. I only knew I felt better. I had learned something very powerful during my year and a half of yoga. I stopped doing and tried *being* more often. I would mindfully stretch my limbs to feel my body. I would stop to breathe consciously. I was doing yoga everywhere without even realizing it. Something inside had changed and my stress level was being reduced. I became more trusting and knew exactly how to slow myself down. I understood now that I had to take care of myself first. *If I am tired and sick, I'm no good to anyone*, I told myself. My attitude toward life had changed significantly. I became more outgoing, more at peace with the world, and more confident. I would catch myself laughing, truly laughing. I was happier.

I had a great summer and I looked forward to going back to my weekly yoga classes, although I found it strange that I was excited about it, since I had struggled with it for so long. However, on my first day back, I had a surprising revelation. The moment my body hit the yoga mat, I experienced an irresistible sense of serenity. My return to yoga delighted and gratified me. Somehow, I felt an instant connection between the ground and my body. I witnessed my breath deepening, my shoulders softening, and my spine lengthening; it was incredible. My body weight literally released itself towards the ground. One by one, my limbs were letting go. It felt as if I was melting into the mat. I even sensed the heaviness of my head and yet it felt light. I was free of the chattering. My usual busy mind had finally found focus. I was present, fully aware of the absolute calmness within my body. For the first time, I understood and experienced Shivasana. I still had some thoughts, but they did not bother me—they were softer and calmer.

At some point in the self-realization, my mind, body, and spirit united as one. I felt a peaceful energy within while experiencing the awakening of every part of my being. I was travelling through my body and had found spiritual awareness. I could see myself from above, looking down, witnessing my body on the ground. I looked so peaceful. I wondered, *If I am up here, then who is down there resting on the yoga mat?* This may sound strange but it was not—it was very peaceful, nothing like the awful symptoms of disconnection or panic I felt when in a state of acute stress. This time I was calm and serene. As I was acknowledging my true self, the spiritual being that I am, I had realigned myself with the power that created me. I felt oneness, I felt God. The divine realization lasted a few moments before the teacher's voice brought me back. I hoped to recreate the great self-realization again one day, so I continued to go to yoga twice a week and started a third day of practice at home.

Through dedication, I received the gift of yoga, and letting go allowed me to feel it deep within myself. During this time, I stopped analyzing and judging everything. I stopped pushing *it* to happen, and amazingly, I stopped being frustrated. My heart knew I had to let go. I had been too caught up in the search, and the moment I let go, the magic happened. Without knowing it, I allowed yoga into my every day life.

> *In a state of yoga, we love everyone and everything, including ourselves.*
>
> —Nancy Forbes
> *Courageous Butterfly*

Today's Reflection

Years ago, I joined Hatha yoga to find peace of mind and freedom from my compulsive thinking. Today, I still do yoga for the same reason, even though my mind has slowed down a great deal.

I live in a body that moves, feels, and thinks. Thinking is part of the human experience; we share stories, create dreams, and design things. I need my mind to express these wonderful things. The mind is a tool for us to use, so when my mind starts acting up, I use my breath to bring me back into harmony—into the present moment.

Now is the only truth we live in.

For a long time, I allowed my ego to control my life, and stubbornly, it fought like hell to keep its power alive. Quieting the mind requires great effort, discipline, and commitment, but my mind didn't want to slow down. It was running twenty-four/seven. In the meantime, the poses of yoga were teaching me to be more attentive. I found myself focusing on my body, noticing my feet for the first time. This is when I understood the true meaning of yoga. I began to realize that yoga is more then just mastering a pose or having a perfectly elastic body. It's about the awareness we bring to the pose. Anyone with a strong flexible body can achieve the end pose. However, if we have not focused our attention on the journey, it does very little for the mind and soul. We may have achieved the pose, but have neglected the inner work. When I first tried yoga, I achieved the end pose quickly. However, I missed the most important act—to move with awareness. I overlooked the step-by-step transitions, the journey, the mind/body/spirit connection.

The physical poses of yoga are exceptionally good for the body. They improve flexibility, strength, endurance, and balance. Yoga brings your entire body into alignment, which improves posture and prevents injuries. The spiritual side of yoga is what keeps me sane, serene, and mentally strong. Yoga teaches non-judgmental awareness of the present moment, allowing us to accept things as they are. True freedom is found in the silence between our words and thoughts. Yoga provides the skills and tools to reconnect us with our source.

When I look at magazines or yoga books, the people promoting yoga usually look like super models with lean bodies, performing beautiful graceful poses. We all have different shapes and body sizes. Who is to say what a perfect body is? Every eye sees its own beauty. A healthy body doesn't necessarily mean a lean body. We have to know that staying fit is not only the need for physical exercises; it takes also awareness, discipline, and commitment. Yoga can teach us moderation, self-discipline, and compassion. It can keep us alert while helping us to stay balanced and strong.

When you are ready, the ego slows down, connecting you to your higher self. From that moment on, yoga becomes a spiritual practice, allowing the practitioner to receive peace of mind, freedom, and union with God. We open ourselves up to feeling a greater sense of harmony with the Universe, inviting beauty from within to radiate into our lives and the world. If your goal is to be emotionally, physically, and spiritually healthy, yoga is one way to achieve it. My life changed significantly for the better because of yoga. The way I think, eat, act, stand, walk, and relate to the world has been transformed. I do not have to think about it anymore; it simply comes, naturally, from the heart.

> *A tulip doesn't strive to impress anyone.*
> *It doesn't struggle to be different than a rose.*
> *It doesn't have to. It is different.*
> *And there's room in the garden for every flower.*
>
> —Marianne Williamson
> *A Return to Love*

Are you struggling with the poses of yoga?

Although yoga poses can be energizing, rejuvenating, and strengthening, it is not about touching your toes or standing on your head. The physical part of yoga is certainly important and can keep us fit. However, if the mind is not at peace, nothing can be achieved—we cannot be happy. I may be proud for a minute or two for completing the pose, but so what? It's just the ego being flattered. I am flexible, and yes, I can touch my toes, but that does not mean I have achieved freedom. It simply means that it is easy for me to do the pose. The person who may arrive halfway into a pose may have used time, alertness, breaths, and gentle efforts. During the act of being present, they went down without forcing or pushing their body into the pose. This student has respected and accepted things as they are and felt freedom on the way. Some people can easily bring their legs around their necks without any effort or awareness. I cannot. It's amazing to watch, but for me this is not yoga. This is simply extreme flexibility. They were born with bodies that can easily move or bend this way. You do not need to reach the ground or wrap your feet around your head to be good at yoga. It's the ego that wants to push so hard, even if the price is hurting yourself on the way there. Forcing the body to arrive in a pose is not yoga. It is competitive, damaging, and stubborn. I have learned from my own experience that yoga can take us to a better place. It may not be standing on your head, but somewhere even more profound, in awareness with the self, with who we really are.

Remember the inner work in yoga is as wonderful and as beautiful as the end pose. To arrive or not to arrive in a pose is beside the point. Being present and honoring the self has a much greater power. To me, yoga is a form of meditation, discovering oneself through great postures—coming into contemplation with *what is*—exploring my feelings with gentle curiosity while becoming acquainted with the physical body as if for the first time. The practice of yoga can be a great learning opportunity, giving us the ability to get to know and respect our bodies, rather than pushing ourselves beyond our limits. The awareness remains with us while we go about our day. We can take yoga into everything we do—for example, washing the dishes, walking, reading. Just being present in what we do is being in a state of yoga.

Even though I am a yoga teacher, I still take yoga classes regularly. It helps me to grow as a student and as a teacher; it keeps me aware and connected. I want to take this opportunity to thank all my students and teachers. Every one of you has taught me something—each and every one of you.

A journey to self-acceptance – A message of hope, love and courage.

From my personal journal

I wrote these words on January 4, 2002

Yesterday I cried in Luke's arms, not tears of sadness, tears of joy.

To my darling Luke,
I'm so blessed to have you in my life, and to have shared with you the wonderful peace I felt *yesterday*; you were genuinely happy for me. I know that you have been really worried about me for the past few years. There is no need to worry, my love, I am feeling better. You are truly my best friend as well as the love of my life, and I trust you completely. Your support and kindness will be forever in my heart. I shall always remember what you have done for me. I truly love you.

To my brilliant son Tyeson,
Tyeson, every mother would be proud to have a son like you. Your kindness, devotion, and most of all, your big heart ... Wow! What a amazing young man you are. Without knowing it, you helped me immensely during the toughest time of my life. All your kisses and hugs gave me the strength to go on. I cannot find the words to express how much I love you.

To my wonderful son Spencer,
Spencer, you are a remarkable young boy, and I love you so very much. *Yesterday*, without knowing it you gave me a sense of peace. Something you said helped me understand my deep sadness. Your trust and faith opened my heart; it was your words that gave me strength and hope. You are nine years old, but there is something about you that makes me think and wonder at your wisdom. You fear nothing and want to know everything.

Yesterday, you helped me realize that Jessy still lives within my heart, and he's forever with us. You know, Spencer, you talk so much about Jessy, I sometimes think he lives through you.

Yesterday, I thought of God again.
God, I'm asking You, how close are You?
Spencer speaks about You all the time; he seems to know so much about You.

To my sweet Angel Jessy,
Jessy, if you can hear me, if you can connect with your brother Spencer, let him know how you are doing. Please let me feel you through Spencer's gentle touch.

Chapter Eight
YESTERDAY, A WISE YOUNG MAN SPOKE...

Think of God as a presence rather than a person.
— Dr. Wayne Dyer

An excerpt from my personal journal
January 3, 2002

We are all students and teachers in life.

Yesterday my teacher was my nine-year-old son, Spencer.

I have been experiencing something amazing lately with my son. I always knew he had a divine connection; however, I didn't realize how exceptionally unique he is. Spencer has always been curious about God, which is strange to me because I never speak of Him. Since Jessy's death, I have lost all faith. Spencer, however, continually asks questions about God. Unable to give him the answers, I decided to buy him a children's bible, which he read twice, and then asked even more questions.

The first sign of Spencer's openness to the source became visible at the age of three. One morning he came to me and said, "Mommy, I want to go home." The strangest thing about his request was that he was home. Many times, he would come to me and say, "Mommy, I want to go home." My answer would be the same one: "Spencer, you are home. This is your home."

A year later, Spencer came to me, lifted up my shirt, pointed at my belly, and said, "Mommy, I want to go home." I could not believe my eyes.

"What are you doing, Spencer? Mommy does not understand what you want." He lifted my shirt again, placed his head underneath my top, and repeated, "I want to go home." I called my husband while Spencer still had his head under my shirt. I asked Spencer to repeat what he wanted while looking at my husband, speechless. This went on for a few more years. One day, Spencer told us he remembered being in my stomach. Wow! This was incredibly amazing and moving. He spoke about the warmth he experienced while being inside me.

Since Spencer was old enough to talk, he would often ask questions about his brother Jessy. Spencer was born five years after Jessy's death, and still he talked about Jessy as if he had known him. In kindergarten, Spencer told everyone he had two brothers, Tyeson and Jessy. Losing Jessy was the worst moment of my life, after which no one spoke of him, including me. It almost seemed as if he never existed. I wanted to talk about him but found it too hard to express how I felt. Now Spencer spoke of him every day. For Spencer, it was natural to talk about him, and I found it therapeutic for me. It forced me to deal with my pain and grief. His innocent way of speaking about his brother made me want to learn more about the other side, so I started buying books like *Healing Grief* and *Talking To Heaven*, by James Van Praagh, *Conversation with God* and *Home with God*, by Neal Donald Walsch, and many more. These books helped me understand the meaning of the grieving process and eventually brought me to self-forgiveness and to God.

I began to wonder how healthy it was for a young child to talk continuously about a deceased brother whom he had never met. I shared my concerns with my husband and decided to take Spencer to a psychologist. The specialist assured us that Spencer was just a very curious little boy. Little did I know that fourteen years after Jessy's death, my son Spencer would bring peace to my deepest sadness.

One day, at the age of seven, Spencer told me Jessy was always around us. "He is our guardian angel, Mom." I loved that idea, our guardian angel. The same day we went out and bought an angel ornament we named Jessy. We hung the angel in front of Spencer's seat in the kitchen. Soon afterwards, Spencer asked if he could keep the angel in his bedroom, so the little angel went to share Spencer's room. Then Spencer started to spend most of his time in his bedroom alone, continuously talking at the top of his voice. It would get so loud in his room that it sounded as if he was speaking with someone else. *Not to worry,* I thought to myself, *he is only playing with an imaginary friend, as most kids do.* I never asked him about the imaginary games he played. I just left him alone. At nine years of age, Spencer moved from his downstairs bedroom to a smaller room on the top floor. This is when the most amazing conversations started.

The late afternoon of January 3, 2002, while Spencer was sitting at the dining room table drawing dragons, I asked him, "Spencer, you don't talk about Jessy anymore, is everything okay?"

"Yes, Mom, I just haven't seen him lately."

WHAT? Did I hear that right? I wondered.

"Spencer, what do you mean, you haven't seen him lately?"

"Since I've moved to my new bedroom, he has only come to see me once."

"Are you telling me that you see Jessy?"

"Yes, Mom. Don't you?"

"No, I don't."

"Ask Tyeson, he knows. Jessy was always with us in our bedroom downstairs." Before Spencer moved into his new room, he had shared a bedroom with Tyeson. I called Tyeson into the kitchen.

"Tyeson, your brother told me that he can see Jessy and you can see him as well."

"No, I don't," Tyeson responded defensively. Spencer screamed from the dining room. "Yes, you can, Tyeson. Jessy was always with us downstairs."

I asked Tyeson to follow me to the living room and asked him again. "Are you sure you don't see him, Tyeson?"

"Mom, I have never seen him, but I believe Spencer does. He always talks to himself. When we go to bed, it's always a one-sided conversation. It's so weird."

At that moment, a change took place in my heart.

"Spencer, how long have you been seeing Jessy?"

"I don't know. I think it started when I was four."

"Why didn't you ever tell me anything before?"

"I don't know. I just thought that everyone could see him. Remember, Mom, when we drove to Montréal and you asked us if we smelt something and I asked you what smell? You said that a scent just passed through that reminded you of Jessy."

"Yes, yes, I remember. I will never forget that scent."

"Jessy was there with us, Mom. Didn't you see him?"

"No. Where was he?"

"Between me and Tyeson."

"OH, MY GOD …" I stopped asking him questions and waited to tell Luke. When Luke came home from work, Spencer joined us in the dining room. I asked him some questions and waited to see my husband's reaction. I then asked my husband what he thought about all of this. "I don't really know what to think, but I do believe him," he said.

I have no doubt what Spencer is saying is true. It's too spontaneous and too natural for him to be making up the story. When Spencer speaks about Jessy, he seems serene, as if I am listening to a different little boy—an angel, perhaps!

Courageous Butterfly

That night, I went into Spencer's bedroom to kiss him goodnight. "Please, Spencer, let me know the next time Jessy comes to visit you. Mommy would love to see him."

Later that week, I again tucked Spencer into bed, but this time I lay down next to him. "Spencer, I want to ask you more questions. I'm very curious about God. Do you know Him?"

"Yes, I do."

"Do you see Him?"

"Yes."

"What does He look like?"

"He has no face, Mom!"

"Yes, He does. We see Him as a man, on television, in pictures, and in books."

"That's not God, it is His son. Don't you know that? You don't see God. You feel Him!"

Wow! I was stunned once again. *Who is this little boy that I'm speaking to? This child looks like a messenger and sounds just like one*, I thought to myself.

"Spencer, why are you here?"

"Because you picked me, Mom!"

"Did you pick me, Spencer?"

"Yes."

"Spencer, do you know what your purpose is?"

"Yes, Mom, to have fun. Everyone is here to have fun. If writing is fun for you, then write. I've been watching you and you seem happy when you write. Whatever you do and love doing, it's your purpose, Mom."

This is incredible! It took me years to figure that one out and hearing it from my nine-year-old ... Well, I was moved.

Whatever makes you feel good is the way to go. Trust your heart. Whenever you feel joy within, you have found your dharma. Stop

113

looking for happiness outside yourself. Whatever resonates with your heart is your true purpose. It's that simple.

Be here, this moment is enough.
Be thankful for what you have *now*.
Love whatever you are doing.
Accept *what is*.
Embrace the simple things of life.
Enjoy your life, Mom! This is what Spencer is telling me.

"Spencer, are you here to help me?"
"No, Mom, I'm here because you picked me."
"Spencer, did God send you here to do something special?"
"Yes, to have fun."

I know now what Spencer means by having fun—living and loving what is.

"Have you seen Jessy lately?"
"Yes."
"When?" I exclaimed.
"A few days ago."
"Remember, I asked you to let me know if Jessy comes back to see you. Why didn't you tell me that you saw him?"
"Because I was having too much fun!"
"Where were you?"
"In my room."
"Where was Jessy?"
"In this corner," Spencer said, pointing to the left corner of his bedroom. "He was behind me, watching me play."
"What does Jessy look like, Spencer?"
"I don't see him, Mom. I just feel him. I just know that he is here."
"What do you do when you know that he is here?"
"I stop playing for a few minutes and look around to see if I can see him."

"Do you see him?"

"No, Mom! I just feel him."

"What do you feel when he is here with you?"

"I feel safe, Mom. I feel good."

"How do you know that it is him if you don't see him?"

"I just know. I just have a strong feeling that he is part of us."

Spencer was getting tired.

"Is it okay if I ask you more questions?"

"Yes, but I'm tired. I want to go to sleep."

I stopped questioning and I kissed him goodnight. I told him that I loved him and that he was a very special boy, and he answered, "I know, Mom."

A smart little guy, isn't he?

I joined my husband in the living room and told him about the amazing conversation I just had with Spencer, and then I wrote down every word I could remember of what Spencer said. The next morning, I asked Spencer if I could ask him more questions.

"No more, Mom. I don't want to talk about it anymore. It's too exhausting."

"But it's about my work."

"Okay, but just one more."

"Can I write about our conversation in my manuscript? I think that we can learn something from it."

"Okay."

"You don't mind if I use your name and write about you and what we talked about?"

"No, Mom. It's the truth!"

"Thank you, Spencer."

Spencer added, "But I would like to read it when it's finished. I want to make sure that it's the way I said it."

"No problem, Spencer, you can read it."

Spencer read it and made me change two words.

What is it that makes children happy? When they play, they play. They live in the moment. They have no worries. They just have fun. Their purpose is playing and their passion is doing what they love to do. This is why they are happy. Unfortunately, when we grow up we tend to forget who we are. We forget how to play. We overlook the true meaning of being here on earth. As Spencer beautifully put it, it's about having fun—not tomorrow, but right now, this moment.

I'm hoping this story inspires you to look deep within yourself, to discover your true passion—what makes you feel good within.

"Yesterday, a wise young man spoke ..." was not originally written for this book. I wrote a program in 2003 on skills and tools to conquer stress, anxiety, and depression. For two years, I hosted meetings out of my house using this program. I wanted to make a difference by sharing what I had experienced, and learned with others.

On May 22 of 2003, I went to one of Wayne Dyer's lectures and he made a statement, which I've never forgotten.

> *"If you are not doing what you love and loving what you're doing, change what you're doing or change how you're feeling about what you're doing."*

When we are truly inspired and living in the moment, we live life through our spirit. *"Don't die with your music still in you,* Dr. Wayne Dyer says.

Play that music and express who you are.
Let the whole world know your dance.

Chapter Nine
THE WHISPERS

By the end of 2002, I had learned to sit quietly with God and I no longer had those terrifying panic attacks. Life was good. I was stronger, stood straighter, and looked taller. The pain I had felt for so many years in my lower back had mysteriously disappeared. Every day I used to have a nap to regain my energy; now I no longer felt the need to do so. I felt revived, and I seriously questioned why I was still on antidepressants. My first attempt to quit was in January of 2003; I believed my new attitude and hard work had healed me, so I gradually discontinued my medication. To help the transition, I made sure I continued with my healthy lifestyle, and yet a short time after, my struggles began all over again. I was nervous, itching, irritable, and impatient. I soon became on edge and very agitated. The hypersensitivities and chronic anxiety was back, and the voices in my head, the fears and worries, had also returned. Even thinking of God couldn't help. I was losing weight and once more became a fragile stick around the house. My life seemed to be moving backwards. It was so exhausting trying to stay mentally healthy. It did not matter how much yoga or positive affirmations I did, my symptoms were back. I was so very disappointed. *What about all the hard work I've done? Doesn't it count for anything?* I thought to myself.

"I know that I can do this," I cried to the Universe. My prayers were not answered as day after day, I continued deteriorating. Yet I still believed that I could do it on my own. I wanted to prove to the world and myself that I could function normally without medication, and so I refused to take antidepressants. I was resisting *what is*, and whatever you resist persists! It got so bad that after a few months I was hospitalized.

I wanted answers, I wanted explanations. *Why is this happening to me again? I did everything I thought possible for my well-being, and yet I still failed.*

Oh, God, this condition is such a mystery to me.

What am I doing wrong? Can you please let my mind rest for just a moment to let me reflect on what happened?

Instead, I was sent to a mental hospital, a terribly frightening place of confusion and chaos. I was in a panic-stricken world. I tried to leave my room, but the other patients frightened me so much that I ran right back in.

This place is not for me, I thought. *Yet if my doctor sent me to a psychiatric ward, does that mean that I am CRAZY? Please, God, give me the strength and courage to survive this heartbreaking setback*, I cried again to the Universe.

Feeling dreadfully angry, I kicked the sheets off my bed and hit the mattress with my fists. I screamed my head off while beating my pillow with everything in me. I was fighting the demons—my terrifying thoughts. If I had been seen, I would have looked exactly like a crazy person. Hours passed and exhaustion took over. I lay my head on the pillow and suffered in silence. Two agonizing days, and not a single doctor came to see me. When finally a psychologist entered my room, she sat close to the door and asked how I was doing. I was still upset and told her the hypersensitivities and anxiety had come back. "I need help and I need answers," I cried. She suggested a higher dose of anti-anxiety pills and left the room. Ten tiny freaking minutes and she was gone. Again I was alone with the inner torment. I was fuming! I don't know what they were thinking, but how could they ignore for so long someone who was suffering? I was already feeling neglected, isolated, depressed, and scared to death.

On the fourth day, I was taken to a meeting room with the other patients. We were asked to fill out papers on how we were feeling, answer questions about depression, anxiety levels, blah … blah … blah. I had already answered all those questions so many times. However, I plucked up the courage, walked up to the front desk, and demanded to leave. I then signed myself out without the doctor's consent. I called a friend and she came to rescue me.

Arriving home was bittersweet. I felt terrible for my children and husband, as they were about to re-embark on a crazy ride once again. In some weird way, being in a mental ward had pushed me to work harder, to recover faster. I knew that with antidepressants, combined with my healthy lifestyle, I would soon get better. Shortly after my return home, my symptoms reduced and my hypersensitivities lessened, decreasing my anxiety. After a few months, I was back to my normal self once again. It was another bittersweet moment. I was thankful for the medication but felt like a failure. I could not understand why I was unable to function normally without antidepressants.

My second attempt was two years later, in 2005. Once more, I felt emotionally ready, as I had practiced the art of silence and yoga for five years, and I believed I was equipped to do it. However, soon after stopping the medication, the hypersensitivities returned, followed by extreme anxiety. It did not matter how prepared I was, I still failed. I had utterly transformed my life by changing my old dysfunctional ways, and yet it was still a struggle to function without medication. During this time, I enrolled in a two-year teacher's training program for yoga with Helen Duquette. The course was demanding, and I sometimes felt overwhelmed with all the homework. I was living a hectic student's lifestyle, and yes, between my housework and motherhood, I had less time to relax or to do things for myself. I was not the only one in the world going to school and being a mother, but it seemed to me that I was the only one having trouble coping with it.

All the way through the program, I was in a better position than most people. I was not working and had time to study, plus, I had a wonderful husband who helped with the household chores. To top it off, my husband also helped me with my homework. I can honestly say that Luke took the two-year course with me because he corrected my English in all the assignments. He also helped me with my reading on the subjects of the history, physiology, and the anatomy of yoga. He patiently explained whatever I did not understand, and occasionally, he would sit on the floor and be my personal student. This is how wonderful my husband is. So what was my problem?

During the course of my training, I gave up some of my meditation sessions. I also gave up reading self-help books. Still, I took the time to do yoga, walk outdoors, and breathe consciously a few minutes here and there every day. Even though the course was taught in English, I enjoyed the program. I studied with passion, and my personal practice and understanding changed a great deal. I realized quickly how much I wanted to become a yoga teacher, but halfway through the course, trying to manage without my medication, my dream was sabotaged. I became sick again; the hypersensitivities were interfering with my studies, and I was losing so much weight that everyone began to notice. No one knew of my past, so they began asking about my weight loss, and the more they asked, the more I became self-conscious. I called Helen and told her my intention was to quit the program. I explained my situation and she was very understanding. She suggested I rest for a while and wait for things to calm down. "Take some time for yourself, Nancy. Get better and come back to us," she said.

Helen was willing to give me space and time to recover, and so that's what I did—and besides, I am not a quitter. I called my mother and told her what was happening and she suggested we go on vacation to Cuba for a week. The antidepressants kicked in after a few weeks and being with my mother on the ocean calmed my nerves. When I came back, I felt stronger. This time, I did not wait until I was completely ruined before taking the medication. However, I could not understand why I had failed once again.

God, why can't I manage normal stresses like everyone else? What am I supposed to do—stay home, meditate, and breathe consciously for the rest of my life? Even that doesn't work.

Two years later, from my personal journal

On February 4, 2007, I went for my usual walk and something incredible happened to me. A gentle Whisper entered my heart. I think it was telling me, *"I love you."*

A chill moved up and down my spine.

Did I hear it right? Where did the Whisper come from?

Soon after, I heard the Whisper once again, but this time a bit more clearly. It softly murmured in my ear, *"I love you. I love you ..."*

This feeling of love was incredible, I was overflowing with joy. It was so powerful that I wanted to cry. It was not the usual voice in my head; this voice was full of kindness and compassion. I could feel, see, hear, and touch it with my whole being. Somehow, I knew it came from a higher power, as if God was talking to me, and I felt blessed. I stopped walking, closed my eyes, and stood still for a little while. I let the moment direct me.

The Whispers continued:
You are not alone.
I am here with you.
I am your friend.
I love you.

"Oh, God, thank you. Thank you."

It felt strange. Imagine God personally talking to you—this is how it felt to me. The moment could have been terrifying, but it was too heavenly to be frightening. I had never experienced this type of love. This love was pure. It came from a place of truth, unconditional and absolute. What a gift!

I opened my eyes and looked to see if anyone was around, but there was no one, I was alone on the street. I started walking again and felt as if Divinity had touched my heart. I walked along peacefully, loving everything and everyone.

The following day, February 5, 2007

I feel an unbelievable closeness with God. In fact, since yesterday He is in me and around me constantly. The Whispers I heard yesterday are a sign, a message from God. This is why I know that today is the perfect day to reduce my meds. I have been on 10 mg for about two years now, which is the smallest dose of my antidepressants. I'm cutting the pill in a half because 5 mg does not exist.

February 9, 2007

The Birth—the day this book was conceived.

I went to bed at 10:30 p.m. and a warm feeling of gratitude came over me. I love this time of the night. I read until I'm so tired that I fall asleep easily.

At 3:00 a.m, my throat felt dry and I was dehydrated. I had dreamt I was drinking continuously but nothing could satisfy my thirst. In the dream, I realized that if I woke myself up, the nightmare would end. I rushed to the bathroom, had a drink, and then went back to bed. My heart was palpitating. Surprisingly, I was not anxious. I was happy and excited; a different type of anxiety was keeping me awake. I was thirsty for action.

Get up and go with it, my heart said.

The Divine Whispers I had heard four days earlier were still vibrating in me, I decided to follow them. I sat on the couch, ready to watch a documentary DVD I had bought the day before. However, before I take you to that chapter of my life, let me tell you what had happened on the previous day. I was getting ready to watch Oprah while preparing dinner for my family. I knew Oprah was interviewing the speakers of *The Secret*. I was in the process of gradually dismissing my antidepressants, and I had been reading books on how to get what you want through the power of visualization. I thought perhaps *The Secret* could help me understand something fundamental about my healing. *How much more is there to the law of attraction, and what is so different about this DVD? The whole world is talking about it,* I thought to myself. It was time; Oprah was on, but halfway through the show, I found myself getting tense. My mind couldn't register fast enough what they were saying; every word they said became an extended thought, and I needed time to process it. I decided to stop making dinner and pay attention to the show—something within was telling me to listen carefully. Just before the show ended, my children came to the kitchen screaming their starvation. They were loud and impatient, and I was getting annoyed. I took some deep breaths and turned the television off, and so my breakthrough had to wait until later.

In the very early hours of a cold silent Saturday, I was sitting on the couch with a pen in my hand, ready to watch the DVD *The Secret*. Even though I really wanted to write, I found myself staring at a blank sheet of paper. I had not written a single word.

I was mesmerized by the documentary, and yet I had unanswered questions. I felt that I had missed something. They had only suggested *ask, believe, and receive*.

But *what about taking action, doesn't that count for anything? Doesn't a Higher Power have anything to do with some of the circumstances of our life? Or do we really have all the power to control every aspect of our lives?* I asked myself.

See, ask, and believe you are driving a new car, receiving a million dollar check, curing your cancer, and it will materialize in your life.

Don't we have to work at it? Or can we just sit and dream about it, and believe it will come to us? Why are they not talking about the importance of taking action after the visualization? Am I missing something?

Am I? Could it be that simple, that easy?

It's now 6:00 a.m.

I'm back in bed, wide awake again. I feel hyper, as if I have had too much caffeine. I'm still reflecting on the words of *The Secret*—pondering what I feel is missing. I don't understand why I feel so strongly about this, but I do.

What is it that I'm supposed to understand? Why do I feel excited and at the same time feel that a piece of my life is missing?

The answer came to me gradually. It came from a place where there is no fear, no game, and no doubt, only truth—my heart.

The Whispers spoke to me: *For two years now, you have lived without your passion. You forgot about your long-time companion, your journal. Writing is your way to express your thoughts and feelings, good or bad, sad or happy; whatever you experience you quickly expressed on paper.*

Suddenly, I remembered my journals and every emotional time and feeling I had written in them. I rushed down stairs and searched. *Where are they?* I wondered. *How many are there?* As I looked for them, I had a vision that inspired me. To my surprise, I had kept them all. I went through every single entry excitedly.

I did not write for the past two years because my focus had been on exploring and remembering where I came from and who I really am. I used all my free time to investigate my thoughts, feelings, and behavior. The words I needed were the ones I highlighted in my spiritual books. During my soul-searching journey, I had come across lots of information, and I had saved many powerful messages, which had been written by spiritual teachers. Whatever resonated and felt true to me, I kept. I was searching and questioning everything. I was on a mission to create my self anew.

On the fateful morning, *The Secret* had awakened my passion to write again. It was time for me to take action. This is why I felt so strongly about the word *action*.

Suddenly, I felt as if something wanted to burst from me, like a birth of some sort. I was ready to bring my newfound understanding to life. My hand was on fire and my heart had a purpose: to create this book.

The Whispers: **Nancy, your story is ready to be shared.**
It is the right time and the right place.
Get up and start writing.

A journey to self-acceptance – A message of hope, love and courage.

First, my heart said, get a thick journal and feel it. *I did.*
Second, the book is yours, you are ready, believe it. *I do.*
Third, visualize your goal, and see it on the screen of your mind. *I did.*
Fourth, take action, and write it from the heart. *I did.*
In my vision, Oprah is the person I chose to share my dream.
Fifth, write a letter to her. Write how you want it. *I did.*
Sixth, now let it go and believe it's on its way. *I do.*
Seventh, be grateful. *I am.*

February 10, 2007

Dear Oprah, I want to share with you what happened to me this week. After watching your show about *The Secret* on February 8, 2007, I decided to take action. The show had awakened my desire to write again. When you read my book, you will understand why I need to share my story. You see, Oprah, I did not believe enough in myself to create what I truly wanted to become. I am a yoga teacher, but I am also a writer. My writing is about real feelings, life experiences, and the gifts that have come to me. Believe me, Oprah, my life was like a soap opera. It's not as bad anymore, since I don't like drama in my life any longer. While my story may be entertaining, I also believe that it has much to give. I'm not famous. However, I am a mother of two and a wife of twenty years with a very powerful story to tell. I lived through extraordinary experiences that have transformed my life. I'm writing this book because I'm hoping to make a difference in someone else's life. I want to share what I remembered, discovered, and learned—that there is only one power in life and that one force is **love**. We have the potential to heal ourselves and to heal the world. **Love** is our hope for a better future.

This dream is helping me to create a new vision—my own yoga studio. I would like to be an instrument of peace. Through my teaching, I want to bring moments of silence, harmony, and joy to others. I want to fund a community center where we can share *love* with one another, being grateful together and collectively delivering positive energy into the world.

Here is a copy of my book.
I am waiting patiently for your response.
Thank you so very much,

Love,
Nancy Forbes

I know the Universe is working at this very moment on my behalf. I am moving forward with my dream. My job is to write my story. Although I am a dreamer, I am not waiting for my book to show up magically on bookshelves. I am now *taking action*.

> *You cannot change anything in your life with intention alone, which can become a watered-down, occasional hope that you'll get to tomorrow. Intention without action is useless.*
>
> —Caroline Myss

February 16, 2007—a week later

I opened the door this morning, but it was too cold to walk, so I decided to go to the gym instead. During my workout, I made the decision to focus only on my breathing. I wanted to experience the full awareness I could obtain, and explore my feelings. I asked myself, *Who are you, Nancy? What do you want in your life?* And this is the answer that came to me:

    I am a divine individual, just as important as everyone else on this earth"

I am unique, I am healthy, I am happy, and I am beautiful.

What I want is peace and freedom.

With every step I took, I breathed in, "I am unique, I am healthy, I am beautiful" and made sure that I felt it with my whole being. "I am a good teacher. I am giving, I am loving ...

"This is who I am. I am all these things."

Before I realized, twenty minutes had passed, and the stepmaster machine stopped. I was back in the room. I opened my eyes and felt empowered. I walked out of the room with a blissful attitude. Everything and everyone around me was vibrating in high spirits. I went on with the rest of my day, feeling exceptionally grateful.

March 1, 2007— two weeks later

It's approximately a month since I decided to quit taking my antidepressants. I don't have any major side effects, except for the occasional tiny shocks in my head. When this occurs, it is dark and I seem to lose a few seconds of time. It's scary, but I know it will pass.

No one knows about my decision to quit my medication, not even my husband. I want to be free of other people's opinions. I don't want anyone to put any doubts or fears in my head. Every morning, I meditate and visualize my healing process. I see it happening in my mind. I rented a video three weeks ago so I could see what a brain and neurons look like. I wanted to see how the brain works. It is so much easier to visualize when you have an understanding of what you truly want. I also bought a book on types of healing one can do with visualization. I do exactly what the book recommends. I asked the Universe to give me the capability of strong concentration, understanding, creativity, intelligence, and peace. I visualize myself having all these things. I make sure I feel it and believe it fully and completely.

Watching *The Secret* really helped me with visualization, for I now have a deeper understanding of the law of attraction.

April 3, 2007—one month later

I'm a little worried, although I'm still very positive. It is what it is. It will pass.

April 6, 2007

I am experiencing sensitivities to noise and smells again. I'm feeling impatient, and I'm losing my cool too often. Every day I use positive affirmations to bring peace and stability into my life. It's work, but I am optimistic that I shall overcome all obstacles.

I am peaceful. I am healthy. I am calm. I am happy. I am blessed. I am grateful. I am … I am … I am. I am all that. I am. I am.

April 8, 2007

This confusion in my life is such a mystery to me. I went to see my doctor again and told him I had stopped taking my medication two months ago. I explained to him that every time I come off the medication, I feel overwhelmed. Every sound and crack turns into a loud irritating echo in my head that doesn't want to stop; light bothers my eyes; and my skin continuously itches. I become quickly impatient, irritable, and anxious. It is constant; it doesn't come and go. I feel this way all day long, and it even disturbs my sleep. My doctor told me other patients have experienced these symptoms as well. He did not know why, but every time the patients attempted to end their antidepressants, they developed hypersensitivities to noise, smells, light, and touch, the hypersensitivities being so intense create the chronic anxiety.

This was very upsetting to me. "I don't want to fail again," I said. "I want to function without these stupid pills. Will these intense feelings eventually go away? I am working right now with visualization," I explained.

He looked at me and gently shook his head, "Nancy, you cannot control this situation with your thoughts. It is out of your control. Do you want to keep fighting, or do you want peace in your life? Do you want to spend your days trying to control the situation? That's a lot of work. Noise is here, all around. Smells will be everywhere, and your skin itches and you are irritated because of it. This is what causes your lack of tolerance. This is why you are anxious and impatient. How many times do you have to go through this? From your past experiences, did the hypersensitivities eventually go away? You found yourself in a hospital because of it. Did you ever think that maybe it is a medical condition, possibly a chemical imbalance, or perhaps a deficiency of some kind that cannot be fixed through visualization or thoughts? Don't punish yourself; you have not failed. Look at everything you have done to change your life. You are a yoga teacher. You meditate and you are healthy. You are also a good mother; you have not failed. See this as someone who has diabetes, who has to take insulin to live a healthy life—they are not failures. They have a condition that is out of their control. If someone is missing a leg, that person cannot bring their leg back through visualization or positive affirmations. Why do you want to suffer and fight this so much?

You have tried three times and every time the hypersensitivities have come back. Go home and meditate on that for a while. Ask yourself, why am I so determined to quit my medication? What is it that makes you think it is so wrong to take medicine that allows you the opportunity to be physically healthy? Nancy, instead of seeing the medication as an enemy, see it as a friendly helper and be grateful for it," he said.

I cried all the way home, deeply troubled. I called my best friend Sasha and told her about my disappointment. She listened patiently without interrupting. When I was finished speaking, she then took over the conversation.

"Nancy, remember who you are. Remember that your soul cannot be touched. You are complete. Your brain is not who you are. It is a tool for you to use. The medicine helps only the part that is challenged in your brain. It does not touch your soul. It cannot touch the part of you that is divine. You have done the work, and you have remembered who you are. You did not fail. Just be thankful for the help. God provided you with what you ask for; this is how he decided to help you. Be grateful for it," she said.

When someone reminds me of God and of His unconditional *love*, everything changes. I change. I hung up the phone and thought about Sasha's words for a while. I sat silently and waited for guidance. But my heart ached with disappointment and I wondered if I could ever fully accept *what is*.

1:30 p.m. on that same day

With a very heavy heart, I decided to go for a walk. I needed to connect with the Earth. I wanted to feel the trees, to hear the birds, to see the sky, and with each step, I felt a bit better.

"Why am I so determined to quit my medication?" I questioned.

This was hard for me to face because I already knew the answer to the question. Being on antidepressants makes me feel like a failure. It makes me feel weak, as if I have a mental illness. It makes me feel incomplete, as if I am cheating or lying. I feel like I am a fake. I'm afraid of what people would think of me if they knew. Would they perhaps think that I am damaged? For over seven years, I've worked hard on my personal growth. I had done lots of inner work. I should be able to free myself of this condition.

I know I am creating my day-to-day life with my present thoughts. I feel like I know this "big secret" and yet, I cannot reach it. I feel let down by life and by myself. I am frustrated and saddened.

Is there a lesson to be learned in all of this? I wondered. *But I'm tired of searching for it. I'm tired of trying to quit. I'm tired of fighting it. I don't want to do this anymore.*

Suddenly the Whispers found their way to me.

Nancy, a pill did not change the way you were thinking, nor did it change your old habits or behavior.

It did not teach you assertiveness or how to manage your stress.

It did not stop you from worrying or anticipating.

It did not teach you how high expectations can be destructive.

It did not inform you about nutrition or exercise.

It did not correct your unhealthy breathing patterns.

It did not bring you stillness or awareness.

It did not remind you of who you are.

<u>*You did!*</u>

You did it all on your own.

A pill is just a pill. It is not a coping skill.

It is not who you are.

It cannot touch your heart.

Accept what is, Nancy, and stop fighting!

Take the smoother road and love things as they are.

You don't need to fight.

You don't need to know why.

Breathe.

Just breathe and trust in Me.

Love who you are.

You are perfect just the way you are.

Everything is perfect just the way it is.

This moment is perfect.

You are perfect.

"Oh, God, thank you!" Suddenly, my heart opened up, and I saw what I had been doing. Living with the thought "still on antidepressants" is living with the belief that I am weak and sick, and that I had failed. I am the one who is judging and being unloving with myself. Oh, God, I need to investigate my thinking further. I need to meet my thoughts with understanding. The thought "still on antidepressants" does not allow me to be free and complete. These three words are making me feel like a failure. Wow! My whole life is on hold while I'm waiting to come off the medication before living my life.

Accepting things as they are and loving who I am is what I need. It will release me from the stress and tension of wanting to be somewhere else in my life. With the full acceptance of *what is* I will then be free of expectations—no more judgment, no more anticipation, and no more disappointment! Free to be me, free to love, free to live my life fully. Accepting things as there are, I trust that what I need is here, right now in my life. There is a reason for things to be as they are. I trust that now. This moment is here to deepen my understanding and compassion, to love and accept myself fully as I am. God has a plan. I trust in that. Something great is coming; I truly believe that. There is a lesson to be learned in *every* moment. This moment is here to teach me self-acceptance, to trust in God's perfect plan—to let go. This moment is giving me what I need to know. Consciously or not, I have chosen this particular challenge to grow. My past prepared me for this moment, and this moment right now is preparing me for my future moments. From this day on, I am forever dropping the negative thought "still on antidepressants." I'm shifting my attitude to one of gratitude. I'm giving myself permission to use God's gift, the medication. This butterfly is courageous, unique, and complete. I am emerging. I am absolute perfection of God's creation. I rest peacefully with that thought.

Wow! What a change! What a difference! I feel so much better.

I do not feel any of those negative things I wrote about myself earlier. I know now that whenever I experience suffering, I can be sure there is a definite thought causing my misery. I cannot change reality, but I can change my experience of it. I have a choice. I can change how I feel. I can meet my thoughts with understanding. I can choose to love. I can ease the pain and stop the madness. I am responsible for my life. God wants to help me, he doesn't want me to suffer or fight for the rest of my life. He has given humans the ability and intelligence to create medicine to ease our sufferings, just one of the ways he provides for us. However, it is up to us if or how we are going to use them. We are in charge of our actions. We have to be accountable for our own health and choices. The responsibility of being informed and making the right choices for our lives is ours. We have that power.

I trust in that.

Chapter Ten
THE EGO SPEAKS HARD

During my third "failure," I wrote down my thoughts—keep in mind that I was in my pain-body, I was suffering.

April 16, 2007

I'm writing this part of my story for the people who have read *The Secret* and experienced strong and painful feelings afterwards. After watching *The Secret*, I went out and bought the book; reading it, I noticed strange feelings returning, feelings that I did not expect to experience, strong feelings of guilt and culpability.

Remember, I was struggling with the symptoms of hypersensitivity during the writing of this chapter.

I thought about *The Secret*,

> *Everything that's coming into your life you are attracting into your life. And it's attracted to you by virtue of the images you're holding in your mind. It's what you're thinking. Whatever is going on in your mind, you are attracting to you.*
>
> —Bob Proctor

But I had never thought I would experience a loss as painful as losing a child.

> *If you see it in your mind, you're going to hold it in your hand.*
>
> —Bob Proctor

I saw in my mind a life with my husband and son Jessy, a happy family and a wonderful life story. Not once did I imagine having such a terrible experience. I dreamed about my son every day, healthy and strong. I was content and grateful. In the end, however, I did not hold my son in my arms.

Then I thought about my healing.

After watching the DVD of *The Secret*, I did the work; I asked and believed, but I did not receive what I wanted. I did not receive healing. All the way through the process, I visualized my healing. I saw the successful outcome in my mind, being free and healthy. I was absolutely certain that I had discovered *The Secret*, and yet the hypersensitivities came back. As the days moved on, I was becoming sicker. I didn't know what I was doing wrong, and yet I knew to focus on good feelings, but they were beginning to dissipate. I had to make a quick choice for myself.

I believed.

I imagined.

I was cheerful.

I am grateful.

And again, I questioned my sanity, my strength, my power, my intelligence, my understanding, and my heart. Where did I go wrong?

I thought about *The Secret* again,

> *It takes no time for the Universe to manifest what you*

> want. *Any time delay you experience is due to your delay in getting to the place of believing, knowing, and feeling that you already have it. It is you getting yourself on the frequency of what you want. When you are on that frequency, then what you want will appear.*
> — Dr. Joe Vitale

There was no doubt in my mind. I believed from the very beginning and with all my heart. I saw the happy ending and I thanked God every day for my recovery.

> *Every teacher in this book uses meditation as a daily practice. It wasn't until I discovered* The Secret *that I realized how powerful meditation can be.*
> — Dr. Joe Vitale

I know how powerful meditation is. I also know it is the perfect tool for visualization, to find stillness, inner space, freedom, and to remember who I am, and to experience God's love. I know this because I am doing it. I am with God every day.

I dragged my restless body outside and went for a walk. It has been six weeks since I quit my medication and I'm not doing so well. The hypersensitivities are driving me insane and I'm anxious every minute of the day. Oh, God, how much power does the law of attraction have on my mental health? Is it truly under my control or is this situation out of my hands? I kept walking, hoping to connect with the Whispers of the Universe. Feeling God's presence, I started to cry, "Please, God, speak to me. I need your guidance." The Whispers: **You have been struggling with the concept of the law of attraction for some time now. You wonder if your destiny is in your own hands or if I have total control of your destiny.**

"When pregnant with Jessy, I was constantly happy. I never thought about him being sick, or worse, that he might not survive. I had no reason to fear. When I was pregnant with Tyeson and Spencer, I then had a reason to fear. It was nerve-racking and I could not see a happy ending. The whole nine months, I was worried sick. Unable to visualize a successful ending, I prepared myself for the worse."

> *When you visualize, then you materialize.*
> *If you've been there in the mind you'll go there in the body.*
> —Dr. Denis Waitley

"What happened to my story?"

The Whispers: **Nancy, Jessy agreed to live a short physical life, and he chose to experience it with you. You both agreed to experience his life and death together for you to evolve and grow spiritually—to remember who you really are.**

Did I choose to experience Jessy's death unconsciously to learn about compassion, love, and be more caring and loving toward others? Yes, it's possible, because this is exactly what happened to me. Yet I don't believe I created Jessy's misery with my thoughts. I don't have that kind of power. I do believe, however, I might have created my depression and panic disorder through my thinking. Jessy's death was such a mystery to me, but since I heard the Whispers I like to believe it was an agreement between God, Jessy, and even the unconscious me. What I am sure about is that life happens, and things happen for a reason.

Death is part of life. Challenges are part of our evolution. They are sent to make us better people. They are here to awaken our spiritual hearts, to connect us to God, to love. When tragedy strikes, does this mean people don't believe enough in a wonderful life? I am a very positive person. I believe with all my heart in having a good and happy life. Still, things happen, good things and not so great.

However, how I perceive "the not so great things" will determine what happens next. If I don't like my situation or how I feel, I can change my experience by changing my perception of it. I can choose to see that what happened in my life had to take place in order for me to be where I am today. Rather than hate it and resent it, I can bless it. I can choose to see my obstacles as blessings rather than a punishment or a life sentence. Obstacles are here to unite us with God, to grow, and to transform us. You may say that I did not believe enough, but I know I did, so is it achievable to receive from asking and believing? Yes, we can; life can be that great. The reality of my story is that my son Jessy left the earth only weeks after his birth, and for now, I need medical assistance to help me with whatever is going on in my brain. All I can do is to accept things as they are and trust in God's perfect plan for me. I certainly can do that.

Today's reflection, a journey to self-acceptance

Eventually I found peace with the law of attraction. A few weeks ago, I again watched *The Secret* and read the book once more. This time I was willing to see it differently. It's my feelings that create my well-being, and not my ego. My ego wanted to heal whatever was going on in my brain so I could look good and prove I was capable of functioning without the help of the medication. What my heart wanted was to feel love and peace. The moment I let go and stopped judging myself and my situation, the transformation began. I received what I truly wanted. My healing simply came in a different form. Love is a state of being in harmony with life. It is the ultimate healing force.

Love is the key to opening the door to freedom; it's the heart that creates heaven on earth. When we choose to love fully and completely, it turns away resentment, anger, and fear. As soon as love becomes the *one* force in our lives, we can truly love life and ourselves, not in a conceited way, but in a divine way. Love is the answer to all things. The love we bring to any struggle has the capacity to change how we see and feel about the situation, therefore changing our experience. I realize we sometimes need difficult experiences in order to grow. In my case, they made me a better person. What we give, we shall receive. I want to love like never before! When we love who we are and where we are in our life, we emerge, we transform. We become beautiful butterflies.

I called the chapter "The Ego Speaks Hard" because my ego was very much present in my writing. I was trying to make the law of attraction untrue, wrong. I did not investigate my thinking deeply enough, because there were still traces of resistance in me, and whatever we resist will persist. If we don't resist it, we take away its power. My past had resurfaced; this is why I felt the way I did during the first reading of *The Secret*. I was defending every bit of my sad story, and I suffered because of it. I now understand that yesterday's suffering was to allow me to grow today, and tomorrow will be the outcome of what I do each day. I am where I am and who I am because of my experiences and my understanding. It was all part of a perfect plan. I did not see it then, but I certainly can feel it now. This experience did not happen to me, but for me. It brought me closer to God, to my soul, to who I truly am.

I'm flying gracefully, I'm flying gratefully.

My guardian angel chose to come to Earth to experience a short life with me. How wonderful this experience truly was! As a human being, I am capable of feeling great joy, love, and compassion, as well as sadness and grief. All of these emotions are gifts from God.

> True power comes
> from accepting things we cannot change,
> and loving *what is.*
> God knows my heart,
> and He knows what He is doing.
> I trust in His perfect plan.
> Everything is the way it's supposed to be.
> Life is perfect!
> Just as it is.
> I trust in that.

I would like to mention at this time two excellent books that were a great influence in my life, *The Power of Now* and *A New Earth* by Eckhart Tolle. In fact, they assisted me on my spiritual journey. I read *A New Earth* over and over again, feeling its words deeply, this book spoke to me. It shook my world and awakened me from my stubborn personality. I finally understood my pain-body and the work of my proud ego. As I read line after line of this powerful book, I felt the dark cloud over my head dissipating and the shadow of fear finally melted away. I could feel layers of my old self peeling away. I took action with my new understanding, and I suddenly felt a light surrounding my being. It was as if God had come to illuminate the road in front of me. It became easier to see things clearly. Through it all, I was reacquainted with the understanding that body and soul are not separate, but interwoven. I also know that *real love* is the recognition of self in others, and there is never a specific thing that I'm supposed to be doing, because my life is unfolding in front of me, one step at a time. I now have a new understanding of my life purpose. Whatever feels good to me is my dharma. When you feel good, you feel God. When you feel God, you feel good. (This is my friend Sasha's favourite way to write the word good; GOoD.) Feeling GOoD, connecting, sharing, and living simply is what I want in my life. When I am living in the moment, I am at my very best. I don't think of the past or anticipate the future, I am fearless. I *love* life. I am at peace with the world and myself.

Another book that made me aware of this is *Loving What Is*, by Byron Katie. Her four life-changing questions called "The Work" taught me how to investigate my thinking and helped me to clarify things. This wise woman believes that there are only three kinds of business in the universe: mine, yours, and God's. For her, the word God means "reality."

> *Reality is God, because it rules. Anything that's out of my control, your control, and everyone else's control—I call that God's business.*
>
> —Byron Katie

Here is what she says:

If I am constantly in someone's business, telling them what they should do or not do, I am living their life. If I am worried about earthquakes, flood, war, or when I will die, I am in God's business.

If I am living someone else's life, or worrying about God's business, than who is living my life? When I am mentally focused on other people or in God's business, I am not present in my own life. Therefore, I am separated from myself, wondering why my life does not work.

She suggests asking ourselves, Whose business am I in mentally? Where are these intense feelings of fear coming from? Am I in somebody else's business?

> *The next time you're feeling stress or discomfort, ask yourself whose business you're in mentally, and you may burst out laughing! That question can bring you back to yourself. And you may come to see that you've never really been present, that you've been mentally living in other people's business all your life.*
>
> —Byron Katie, with Stephen Mitchell
> *Loving What Is*

Storms and tornados are part of life; they happen without our consent. Like the weather, humans go through some rough and wonderful times. It pours, it rains, it shines … and yes, there are things I cannot control. However, I can control my actions. I can meet my thoughts with understanding and therefore see the Truth. My present thoughts, behaviors, and decisions will determine what happens in my day-to-day life. I have that power. When hard times hit, I may not be able to change the reality of them, but I can definitely change the experience. I can investigate my thinking, and change how I feel.

I ask myself these four questions, by Byron Katie
1. *Is it true?*
2. *Can you absolutely know that it's true?*
3. *How do you react when you think that thought?*
4. *Who would you be without the thought?*

I would like to add to the list,
Where would you be in your life without that thought?

Thoughts that cause pain:	My friends don't respect me.
	I am wounded, no one cares.
	I can't trust anyone, life is hard.

Now, investigate each thought. Is it true? Can I absolutely know that it's true? How do I react when I think that thought? Who would I be without the thought?

I asked myself, where would I be in my life without that thought? I discovered that without that specific thought, I would be moving on with my life peacefully, happily and in love.

Following Byron Katie's four questions, there is a "turn it around" exercise that I found very powerful. In her book, Byron Katie does an excellent job of illustrating the exercise step by step. She writes:

> When you become a lover of what is, there are no more decisions to make. In my life, I just wait and watch. I know that the decision will be made in its own time, so I let go of when, where, and how.

I now know how to live my life and be whoever I want to be. I am doing it. If I don't like a situation in my life, I can change it by changing how I feel about it. I can choose to love fully and completely. I can ask myself, *what is the worst thing that can happen*—knowing that the worst can never be that bad, as God has a better plan for me.

Accepting *what is* does not mean that I have given up or that I stop improving my life. So what does it mean?

To me, it means understanding and then dropping the thoughts that cause me pain. It means letting go of thinking that I have failed. It means living the moment as it is, and knowing it is, the way it is because it just is. It means going on with life without thinking that it should be this way or that way. Such thoughts keep us trapped in frustration and depression. It makes us feel like failures, not good enough. Living with *what is* means trusting in the Universe, in God's work.

Each moment has its purpose. I may not be able to see it right now, but this moment right now is perfect just the way it is. There is a reason for this specific moment to happen.

I trust in that!

Courageous Butterfly

There is a time to suffer,
and there is a time to fight and survive.
Now, it is time to let go and let God.
Love *what is,* and if you cannot,
then learn to accept it.
It is *what is!*
Flow with it.

Today, I know about finding *my* Truth, and it's the most essential part of my healing. When I walk my own path, I am true to myself, and I am with Spirit. For many years, I have read, studied, listened, and tested what I have learned. Whatever a friend, teacher, or book suggested, I tried. I love reading spiritual books, going to retreats, and listening to great teachers speak about life, but I always go back to the voice within me —*my heart.* My heart is the radar that will tell me whether it feels right or true to me. A few weeks ago, a friend (who holds seminars on the law of attraction) asked me if I was still struggling with the desire to quit taking my 5 mg of antidepressants. My answer was no, I'm accepting and loving *what is.* She then told me that it did not work because deep down I did not believe enough. She said, "You said that you did, but your subconscious did not. You need to change that part of yourself." Wow! That was a slap in the face and it hurt, but I only allowed it to hurt for a few seconds. I knew I hadn't failed. She may have been right about the subconscious thing, but my heart felt differently. My heart told me to stop fighting and to accept things as they are—it's that simple. I don't need to prove anything to anyone, including myself. This is my story, and I choose to live my life the way I want it to be. Loving *what is,* this is what I want. God is providing for me, and I choose to stop fighting. I choose freedom. I refuse to fly against the wind any longer, it's too hard and exhausting, and besides, it has taken me nowhere. This time, I will let the wind carry me. I'm following my heart. I'm traveling with God.

Fly Little Butterfly

Even a caterpillar can learn how to fly,
so fly, little butterfly. Fly!
All caterpillars have the potential
to transform themselves into beautiful butterflies.
They may resist change;
being uncomfortable with *what is,*
they doubt their ability to fly.
But if they surrender to *what is,* nature does its work
and the transition happens gracefully.
All caterpillars spin a cocoon wherein they wait in silence.
It's dark; however the process is a necessary one—
without it, they wouldn't see the light and soar into the sky.
In sunlight, they emerge peacefully,
and harmoniously rise with the highs and lows of life.
They become who they were meant to be—beautiful butterflies.
So fly, little butterfly. Fly!

Since my life is shaped by my present thoughts, may I love, trust, and see beauty in myself and others, and everywhere. Through the grace of an open heart, may I see the world as *one,* rather than *fear* the world.

I read somewhere that Spirit does not have to search for happiness. Spirit has it all. It is supreme wisdom, and Life itself. It rests in harmony and gives love freely. Spirit is joy. It's what keeps us going. It's the light of our path, the faith of our hearts, the purity of our thoughts, and the beauty we see in others and ourselves. Spirit keeps us connected to kindness, joy, and blissfulness. It keeps us whole and complete as we travel through life. Spirit never dies; it remains with everyone we have touched and loved. Spirit is the gentle voice in our hearts that reminds us that we are loved by God, never alone.

> *Ironically, the Buddhist view is that the mind is located in the middle of the chest. An open heart is an open mind. A change of heart is a change of mind.*
>
> —The Dalai Lama
> *An Open Heart*

The inspirations from Heaven are the best advice and ideas I ever had. When we think from the heart, we are open to the Whispers of the Universe, and we create from the soul. A hunch or a deep feeling is our guardian angel talking to us. It says, "Before you even think of asking for what you want, sit quietly and meet your thoughts with understanding, listen to the voice of your soul, and then ask and believe. Life will bring you the right experiences; trust in that. Divinity will bring you the right inspirations; be sure of that. Together you are creating your story, and your success will be the manifestation of your intentions, inspirations, and actions. Your job is to keep on trusting and believing."

> *As I reflect, I'm mirrored in the light of others; I see myself in everyone.*
> —Courageous Butterfly

A journey to self-acceptance – A message of hope, love and courage.

When thinking from the heart, the mind opens up to love and compassion. Kindness, patience, tolerance, generosity, and prosperity all come from an open heart and spreads out into the world with a grateful mind.

I realize that not once over the past seven years did I ask for financial prosperity. I had lost the desire to be financially successful—don't get me wrong, I still appreciated nice things, I just didn't have the desire to be rich anymore. Money was no longer the main concern of my life. I discovered that true success is love, peace and joy. It doesn't rest with money or power, it's waking up in the morning feeling excited about life, about what I want, and what I can do today. I realize money is great to have, it's a good tool to use to get the things I need and love in my life. I would like to travel and see the world; money would also be another way for me to give back and make a difference somehow, somewhere. To find balance is what I truly want. I'm open to prosperity in every area of my life.

Balance is the key to a joyful life.

When I am rigid, it is difficult to balance.
When I am too loose, it's hard to have a sense of equilibrium.
When I shift too far in one direction, it's hard to find stability.
But when I become aware of my feet, I have security and strength.
I feel the ground, and I know balance is not too far away.
With a strong foundation, my spirit can fly high.
Successfully, I am.

I wondered if I should keep this part of my story in this book. Initially, after reading the following stories, I felt I was sounding like a great teacher who knows all the answers. Believe me, *I am not*. I am simply a forty-eight-year-old woman who decided to write her story, and by doing so, I hope to connect with the world. These stories are part of my personal growth; they are about my *own* reaction to life and pain. Originally, I did not write them for this book. However, I have many interesting stories, and I realize each of them has a purpose in being told, as my book is meant to be inspirational. One day during a moment of crisis, I opened my journal and began to read the short stories I had written. The writing was scribbled and hard to understand, but after unravelling it, I noticed I felt better. I sat in front of the computer that night and began to rewrite the entries that appear at the back of this book.

Years ago, I started a routine of investigating my thoughts, and when I felt sad or lonely, I went within and asked God for guidance. It was during my daily walks that I noticed a miracle happening—being outside in nature altered my state of mind. I felt more alive and connected to the Universe; these walks turned out to be part of my spiritual awakening. Before long; my heart began to speak to me. It was as if the words I highlighted in my spiritual books came alive. They spoke to me in the form of Whispers.

Keep in mind that this is *my story*. However, if these stories speak to you, please use them, please use whatever resonates within your *own* heart. If nothing resonates with you, delete them, or just enjoy the experience of reading. My heart is telling me to share them with you, and so I shall.

In my newfound and profound awareness, an answer came to me, a new vision appeared, the Whispers spoke once more, letting me into the light, and my fears and anxieties disappeared.

PERSONAL MESSAGES

> *When we are no longer able to change a situation - we are challenged to change ourselves.*
> —Viktor E. Frankl

I was never truly lost, just dormant, when a spiritual call shook my world and yoga entered my life. I witnessed again and again the truth of the statement, *When the student is ready, the teacher will come.* I believe this relates to books as well as human beings.

As cliché as it sounds, yoga changed my anxious personality to a calmer, trusting one. It has affected me positively in so many areas of my life. It has influenced the way I eat, think, act, and even my reading. I read now with my heart. When I first started yoga, I did it merely with my head. I performed the same neurotic behavior throughout my life, as my mind could not connect with my heart as one. That is why I judged and analyzed everything, and this is why my life did not work. I was separated from my source. I realize now that it is one thing to move through life with my head, and it's quite another to do so with my heart. When I read with my head, the information stays in my head. I do not feel the information with my whole being. Therefore, I do not experience it in my life. It's the heart that makes the difference in our journey, because the heart understands the information at a much deeper level. It connects the mind to *love*. It connects us to our *spirit*. With time, yoga has moved me to a higher level of consciousness, my heart. I became inspired and intuitive, while in the midst of self-recognition, I became aware of the *love* inside me. I wanted to experience love in all of its glorious ways, and so I decided to live my life with an open heart. I wanted to be more compassionate, loving, trusting, grateful, and disciplined. I wanted God in my life.

Today, whenever I read a book, I make sure I have an open mind and heart. I welcome the opportunity to receive insight with my whole being. Every book I choose has a purpose, a personal message. It could be small, big, new, or old, it doesn't matter. I have never read a book without finding a meaningful message, and some of these messages I have included in this book. Although I may already know some of the wisdom, it is always good to hear it again. I pause with what resonates with me, allowing the message to do its work. I always read with the intention of receiving a gift and I always do. I'm so thankful for the great teachers in this world who have written books, they have assisted me in my divine awakening.

A personal message

To me, I feel each message right in my core and soul. It is something that feels true to me; truth exists in my heart. Books, people, and things outside of me can only guide me to *my* truth. My instinct cannot fail me; I'm where I'm supposed to be. No one's path is better than anyone else's. There is a divine purpose behind every struggle, every obstacle, and every kindness. All things are happening in divine order and with perfection.

All along, my writing has released the voice within me; things happen for a reason. My writing had more meaning than just keeping a personal journal—it was to lead me to a greater purpose in my life, to free me from my irritability and depression. My gratitude on paper became something much bigger; it nursed me back to health. Through it all, I discovered that my feelings are within my control. I decide how to react and think about life. I have that power. Lately I have noticed a difference in the intensity of my emotions. Even though I still get angry and sad at times, there is now a *calmness* within the emotion. The great sadness does not have to be so sad, and life does not have to be so hard.

We are not human beings having a spiritual experience.
We are spiritual beings having a human experience.
—Pierre Teilhard de Chardin

I am a divine individual experiencing life. I'm evolving, discovering, and remembering every day, and in the course of this incredible journey, I have learned that life is a process, a step-by-step development. Therefore, I don't want to reject my ego as it is part of the whole—God's creation. I can learn to understand *it*— so it will become my friend. Every part of me is a masterpiece of God's creation, and every part of you has been designed by God's hand—also a work of art. We truly are perfect.

The path we choose in life is ours, as we have free will. There are numerous roads we could take—the long and hard road, the road of denial, the victim's road—but there are also smoother roads, simple roads—the loving road, the forgiving road, the grateful road. It is up to us; we choose our path. It's never too late to change a path. We choose what to experience. This is what my therapist meant when she said, "Nancy, no matter which road you take, you cannot fail to arrive home." We are *all* returning to where we came from, no matter which path we take. I had unconsciously chosen a hard and painful road during the first half of my life. Today, I'm making the conscious decision to change my path. I'm choosing to walk an easier road, the road with God, to peoples' hearts, to love, to yoga, to connect with nature and the world.

Wow, I just had a "ah-ha" moment—it doesn't matter which path I decide to take in this life, I cannot fail to arrive home, to meet God, because God had never left me. He is always and forever within *me*. I am home—we all are. God is within us always and forever, we just need to sit quietly long enough to experience Him, to feel Him. I feel in my heart that we are here to help each other to remember, to awaken. The road we decide to take in this life is not to return home, it's to remember where we came from, who we really are: *"One with God,"* like so many great teachers have said and still say today.

I surrender to the Higher Power who created me; this is the road I decided to travel in this life on earth. What road do you choose to travel?

THE MONKEY MIND

> Today is a gift,
> and that is why we call it The Present.
> Yesterday is history, it's just a story.
> Tomorrow is a mystery, lost in obscurity.
> I choose the Present—God's light.

I've let my anxious mind run my life for over thirty-seven years. It was not until I truly started living in the present that I began to understand the depth and importance of being in the moment. In time, I began to realize that thoughts are just mental movements passing through the mind. They are not facts, they are not me, they are only thoughts, and often giving false impressions and hallucinations. Listening to students who share their thoughts with me, and from my own experience, it seems the mind loves to be preoccupied with the past and concerned with the future. The ego is uncomfortable with silence; it does not like to be in the present moment. It constantly needs entertainment, drama, and confrontation. I called this insane behavior the monkey frame of mind, jumping from one thought to another, always searching for a better place to be, or it settles for the past. It often craves for things to be different or the way they used to be. When I identify myself with the monkey mind, I feel the pain of the past, or again, the fear of anticipation, resulting in suffering. The intensity of suffering always depends on the degree of resistance with the present moment. What I think, I feel. If I think about the pain of the past, I feel awful. The body does not know the difference between things real and imagined. When my brain sends messages of danger, fear, or hatred, I feel as if my body is under attack. I become anxious and depressed.

Whenever my mind travels to the past, I lose sight of the present moment, and as my mind gets into the monkey mood, I become absorbed by the past as if I was truly there, and wherever my mind is, there I am!

I started this life with a clear mind with zero information. Then I picked up ideas, beliefs, and baggage on the way through life that made me feel bad about myself and the world. Unfortunately, intense fear is what I knew in the past. When fear enters my life, I recognize it as irritation, anger, confrontation, and pain. I have learned how to stop it; I use my breath to take me to my roots, to God. God created us. We are born in perfect love. We are made of love. Therefore, we are love. There is no reason to fear, fight, compete, hate, or suffer. At any time, I can investigate what is truly going on in my head and see the truth. When I meet my thoughts with understanding, I find clarity. I have the choice to end the madness or keep on believing the insanity that my mind creates. It's easy to perceive life with fear, (judging, accusing, assuming), entering into the darkness that the mind creates. When we love, we shine. We can face our fears and replace them with love. Every moment we take with our breath is a true moment of healing. We see thoughts for what they truly are—not facts, but simply mental movements. This way, we let our hearts speak. Fear comes from the mind that is disconnected from God. I cannot have God in my life and have fear too. I choose God. I choose to love.

Living in the moment, I sense that there is something more powerful out there. At first, I questioned it, and then I was drawn to it. Once I found a certain degree of presence, I recognized the divine essence living within all. With the help of the CD *Getting in the Gap*, by Dr. W. Wayne Dyer, I learned that I could create space in my mind. I can do this by visualizing a gap between my thoughts; I see myself resting in that space. At that moment when I feel a deep connection to God, a profound sense of belonging comes to me, where peace and joy is experienced, and where *love* and divine inspiration resides.

If you breathe consciously, you will know you cannot think and be aware of your breath at the same time. However, we can experience and feel God. We are honoring the power of *now* and have put the monkey mind to rest. Suddenly, we are moving through life with ease. We have aligned ourselves with the Universe, with the great power that created us, God. When we stop to smell the roses, we can see beauty everywhere in all things. A few conscious breaths every day prepares the mind to see clearly, loving the wonder of now. When the mind is free of disturbance, it receives information through the antenna of the soul. Insight and inspiration will directly come from spirit awareness, the voice of God. Believe it, freedom is never too far away.

If you really want to know how stubborn you are, just approach the idea of being willing to change. We all want to have our lives change, to have situations become better and easier, but we don't want to have to change. We would prefer that they change. In order to have this happen, we must change inside. We must change our way of thinking, change our way of speaking, change our way of expressing ourselves. Only then will the outer changes occur.

—Louise l. Hay
You Can Heal Your Life

THE TRUTH

All the world's a stage, and all the men and women merely players.
—William Shakespeare

Inspired by the Whispers:

What is Truth? Is there such a thing as one Truth? So many people think they have found the Truth. I believed I knew the Truth. All my life, I was convinced I had all the answers; now, I don't know. I only know that *my* Truth is simply a story, my story.

The world is as I perceive it to be! I lived most of my life in fear, and from that perspective, I believed I knew the Truth. I was naive and misinformed. My beliefs could not have been further from the Truth. How can it be Truth if I am moving through life with anger, depression, anxiety, and unawareness? When my mind was disturbed by the past, I blamed my life situations, my parents, and even God for my misery. The Truth was the sad story I believed in. When the Truth comes from a broken heart and painful memories, we are blinded by sorrow and anger. How can we know Truth when we respond and re-act out of resentment and bitterness? When I am convinced that I know the Truth, I become rigid and life becomes hard. Moreover, when I look at life through eyes blinded by stubbornness, I judge, accuse, fight, resist, and suffer.

A journey to self-acceptance – A message of hope, love and courage.

In that moment, everything changes for you. Nothing is the same anymore, because now you see what's really happening. People live in their own world, in their own movie, in their own story. They invest all their faith in that story, and that story is truth for them, but it's a relative truth, because it's not truth for you. Now you can see that all their opinions about you really concern the character who lives in their movie, not in yours. The one who they are judging in your name is a character they create. Whatever people think of you is really about the image they have of you, and that image isn't you.

— Don Miguel Ruiz, Don Jose Ruiz
The Fifth Agreement

Humans have a powerful imagination; we are storytellers.

Here is what I understood from *The Fifth Agreement*, a wonderful book by Don Miguel Ruiz and his son Don Jose.

The mind is so powerful that it perceives the story that we create. Humans tell themselves stories every day. We create either Hell or Heaven; both are states of mind that exist within us. When we create Hell, we are either at war with the world or ourselves; it's a battle between ideas, opinions, and beliefs. Believing in lies is how we create our own nightmares. On opinion is not Truth, it's just a point of view; assumptions are not Truth, they are imaginary tales; superstitions are not Truth, they are fears, distorted stories. Gossiping or judgment—he is too short, she is stupid, I am not good enough—is not Truth, it's a language of injustice and punishment. These stories are nothing more than lies that we are telling ourselves.

They have nothing to do with Truth. They are simply things we make up, stories we believe in.

> *We put our faith in lies; we give them life, we give them power, and soon those lies are ruling our lives.*
> *That is why it was said that every head is a world, because each of us creates and entire world in our head, and we live in that world.*
>
> —Don Miguel & Don Jose Ruiz

This book of wisdom tells us that lies only exist if we create them, and they only survive if we believe in them. Fear, anxiety, misery are nothing more than stories full of lies.

Complaining and finding fault in others or in situations are just forms of wanting to be right. Would you rather be right or at peace? I learned a very powerful affirmation from Dr. Wayne Dyer's book, *There's a Spiritual Solution to Every Problem* —a line he borrowed from *A Course in Miracles*. "I can choose peace, rather than this." Then he continues; "it is a terrific reminder to recall in moments when we are not being an instrument of thy peace."

"I can choose peace, rather than this."

Here's another powerful statement that shook me.

> *There is nothing that strengthens the ego more than being right. Being right is identification with a mental position—a perspective, an opinion, a judgement, a story. For you to be right, of course, you need someone else to be wrong, and so the ego loves to make wrong in order to be right. In other words: You need to make*

A journey to self-acceptance – A message of hope, love and courage.

others wrong in order to get a stronger sense of who you are.

—Eckhart Tolle
A New Earth

Wow! That feels so true. The ego loves to make others wrong in order to have a sense of superiority.

We have the choice to fight or surrender, to hate or love, to blame or forgive. Would I rather be right or at peace? I choose to be free. I choose peace. When I drop the desire to be right, a transformation begins. I see the world differently. I am at peace. I stop trying to prove that I am more or better than anyone else. I am no longer trying to fit in or worried about what other people think of me. I let go of superstitions, assumptions, and lies. Why not start from the ground up? Every flower begins to grow from the earth. When I stop to feel the earth beneath my feet, I discover its power—the stillness of the present moment. I have a strong connection, I'm grounded, and I'm aware of the Light in me. I accept all of me, the part that is good, the part that is dark, the part that is challenged, the part that is loving, caring, charming … and so I let go and grow. I remember where I come from and let God direct my way. All I can do is to grow one moment, one foot, and one step at the time. When I'm open to receive the energy of the earth, I blossom like a colourful flower. I become beautiful.

> I am beautiful.
> I am everything in everyone.
> I am the best. I am the worst.
> I am nothing more and nothing less.
> I truly am.

Everything I have written in these pages is my experience; it's only my story, therefore my truth. Whatever makes me feel peaceful and happy *today* is my truth. Walking in nature and expressing myself through writing and music is my truth, as it brings me great joy. Yoga and meditating is also my truth, as it keeps me grounded, connected, and peaceful. I have a mind now that is open to everything, and a heart that wants to love a whole lot.

Having an open mind is a choice we make. Remember, an open heart is an open mind. We can make the conscious decision to love fully and completely, and we can also send out into the world the *love* that's been awakened in our hearts.

> Peace begins within us.
> As a new day begins, release your spirit from yesterday. When we give the past more attention than the present, we lose our power to create a better tomorrow. Find harmony in the stillness of the present moment, and let only the wisdom and love from the past serve us.
> The world needs you. I need you.
> Allow the beauty within you to shine each and every day—let the world see your light and through the light of your example, others will see their light—the world will glow and its people will radiate love.
> We can make a difference—a better world for our children.
> I know we can, because my soul is telling me so.

I awake every morning feeling excited, as my heart leads me on a new path each day. When my Spirit is present, everything in my life is better. I travel through life with joy and ease. The heart is our connection to Truth, and my heart wants to love, explore, remember, and share great joy. When the voice within us speaks—there is Truth, harmony, peace and joy.

In the presence of fear, anger, or sadness we have to ask ourselves if we really want to stay in that state of mind—of course the answer is no. We then have the option to meet our thoughts with understanding, and by bringing awareness to the negative emotion, we feel it, we recognize that fear, anger, and sadness are the result of our thinking. We have the choice to replace the thought of fear, with a thought of love—our experience will instantly change. This is a conscious choice, of course, and a great solution to bring light into the darkness. We know that there are only two emotions, fear and love, and we are free to choose. When we choose to love fully and completely we stop fighting and truly live. We experience the full wonder and magnificence of who we really are and why we are here. *Love* is the highest state of being, and it's available to all of us if we make that choice. Choose to love, choose to make a difference—make our world a better place. Remember, however, it all begins within us *first*.

> *There is no truth except the truth that exists within you. Everything else is what someone is telling you.*
>
> *I did not say that nothing exterior to you can lead you to your truth. I said that you are the only one who can take you there.*
>
> —Neale Donald Walsch
Home with God

CLOSENESS WITH GOD

Reach high; reach for the stars.

From my personal Journal, August 7, 2007

When I walked this morning, I thought about my book. I have been writing for six months and I know in my heart I'm doing exactly what I'm supposed to be doing. However, for the past little while, I have wanted to share the excitement I feel with somebody. It would be nice to have a strong spiritual bond with a special someone during the writing of this book, to share my thoughts and dreams and radiate the love and happiness I feel inside. I'm fortunate to have many people I trust in my life—two of these people are exactly who I'm looking for. A few weeks ago, I asked both of them if they would like to co-write the book with me. Both considered my offer and then they declined for personal reasons. I was heartbroken; they seemed so excited when I first suggested the idea. I also felt rejected, as if it was something personal about me. This caused me grief, so I took a moment to investigate my thinking and realized their decision had nothing to do with me. I know everything happens for a reason. There had to be a bigger picture for me out there. I kept walking, and asked God to help me find someone special to work with me on this book. At first, it was difficult to consider anyone else. I dismissed the thought and decided to surrender my idea to the Universe.

"I trust in You," I softly murmured out there.

I heard the Whispers say, *Nancy, you are already co-writing this book with a special someone. Don't you feel it? Don't you see it? This special someone you are looking for is Me, Your Friend, God. I am everything you are looking for. I am trustworthy, honorable and I radiate pure Love.*

I wanted to cry. *You remembered who you are. You have found Me. You can share your thoughts with Me, and I will be right here listening to your hopes and dreams. We can discuss life together, share visions, share feelings, and talk about anything. Don't you see? I am the perfect partner to co-write this book with you. My love is unconditional. You can trust in that.*

"Oh, God, I trust in You. You are the perfect partner. I'm co-writing this book with You, because I am co-creating my life with You."

The Whispers: *I have been here all along, walking with you, but you couldn't see Me. Your mind was too busy looking for someone outside yourself. Only you can write your book. This is your story, your experience, your understanding, it's your life.*

"Oh, God, I was blinded by desperation. I've always had the perfect partner."

"It is You. I see it now. I'm writing my life with You. You and me, me and You, always and forever, eternally and for eternity."

"Please allow me to summarize Your perfect plan. You planted the seed within me long ago, the writing of my journals. You knew we were going to do this together. You knew exactly what experience, lessons, and understandings I should have so I could write about them today in this book. I agreed to experience the pain and the joy of my story without being aware of it. Wow, my story is truly unfolding one step at a time."

"I was not aware of You then, but I am now."

"I know now that when things do not go my way, it is because You have something better in mind for me. I trust in You."

Sometimes the Soul chooses things at a subconscious or a superconscious level that it would never choose at a conscious level, and that it does this in order to fulfill its Larger Agenda.

Have faith in God's perfect plan.

—Neale Donald Walsch
Home with God

"GOD IS LOVE, LOVE IS GOD."

> *The soul is nothing more than an Individuation of Divinity... and it is absolutely nothing less.*
> — Neale Donald Walsch

August 16, 2007

Wow! Something wonderful happened to me this morning. I went on my usual walk and decided to use a mantra to keep me company.

My mantra was as follows:

I honor the divinity that lives within me.
I honor the divinity that lives within me.

While repeating the mantra, I felt lighter on my feet, and joyful in my heart, and so I kept repeating it.

I honor the Divinity that lives within me.

The more I repeated the mantra, the more blissful I became. Everything around me seemed more alive. Trees appeared greener, the sky was brighter, birds sang more beautifully, and their melodies nourished my heart. It was unbelievably empowering.

Without realizing it, my mantra changed.

I honor the individuality that lives within me.
I honor the individuality that lives within me.

I kept walking and repeating the mantra and began to feel a great appreciation for who I am as a human being. My personality is unique, my desires are unlike anyone else's, and my special talents are exceptional. Wow! I love who I am. I am a unique individual and at the same time, I am equal to everyone.

We have the *same* Father, God.
We have the *same* Mother, Earth.
We all breathe the *same* air and use the *same* soil, made up of the *same* energy.
Wow! We share the *same* breath.
There is no separation between us.
We are One and the *same*, but different.
We are individuals, having distinctive personalities, yet still the *same*.

I have no way of articulating what was happening to me. I just continued walking along the river road while experiencing a greater understanding of myself.

I honor the divinity and individuality that lives within me.
I honor the divinity and individuality that lives within me.
Suddenly, the "me" changed to us.
I honor the divinity and individuality that lives within us.
I honor the divinity and individuality that lives within us.

I felt uplifted and united with all. I had never experienced the power of *love* that strongly before. I was in love with everything and everyone. Just like that, I started whispering, *I love you*, to every living thing I saw on the street: trees, birds, squirrels, chipmunks, cats, dogs, etc. Suddenly, I noticed two fawns crossing my neighbor's backyard. How wonderful! I was truly blessed.

If I met someone on the street, I murmured softly in my heart, *I love you*. It did not matter what race, color, nationality, or sex they were, I loved them all! I knew I was connecting to everyone and everything in a deeper level of consciousness, my heart.

Oh, God! I was in love with the whole world and the entire

Universe. It was INCREDIBLE! I was vibrating pure *love*. What a healing sensation that was! I was free to love openly and completely.

Wow! I think I'm having a relationship with God.

No, I *know* I am having a relationship with God.

A few months later

I was in the car with my husband driving silently home when suddenly I felt an urge to share my gratitude. I felt extremely joyful for no specific reason. I stared out the window, my eyes following every person on the street. This was the second time that this intense feeling to share the power of *love* with everyone and everything had occurred. I tried to make eye contact with each person on the street, but it was almost impossible. My body turned in every direction. I was on a mission to reach peoples' hearts. I began whispering, *I love you.*

My husband looked at me and said, "Nancy, what are you doing?"

"I'm trying to connect with everyone," I said. "I want them to know that I love them. I'm whispering, *I love you*, to everyone I see on the street. Try it, babe, it feels so good. See how empowering it is. You will feel revived and your heart will fill with joy." I kept doing my thing and Luke kept driving silently.

I noticed a man walking and looking down at his feet. His back was arched forward, and he seemed sad and lonely. I thought if I could reach him for a moment, if he could receive my love and compassion, maybe his heart would open up to hope, to the Whispers of the Universe. Maybe he would feel GOoD and rise up to a true moment of Joy. Suddenly I remembered the day I heard the Whisper, *I love you,* for the very first time. Those three little words had changed me forever. They are in me, with me, and around me constantly. They are the words of God—a *gift* from the Universe. It may seem that I received something small and simple, but in fact, I received something exceptionally powerful. Amazingly, it was something I already had within me. When I say *I love you*, and listen to its magical resonance, I feel God's presence, and that is the reason it feels so good. Saying *I love you* for no specific reason, to no particular person, on no special occasion is empowering, awakening, and healing. It evokes the spirit of *love* within and transforms the energy around us. Yet it all begins within—whatever I experience in my life, I experience first within me.

It is so exhilarating. I found another simple wonder of my life—the act of saying *I love you* to whoever comes my way. I can see myself spreading the power of love all over the world.

I love you.

We speak of the world as One.
God created everything and everyone.
We are the offspring of the Universe.
God is our Father.
Earth is our Mother.
We are divine, children of the Universe,
sisters and brothers under the sun,
one gigantic family.
We just need to sit still long enough to experience it, to feel it.

THE GREATEST GIFTS

Out of my greatest despair was to come the greatest gift.

—Rhonda Byrne
The Secret

What a powerful and astonishing sentence this is! *Out of my greatest despair was to come the greatest gift.* I can truly understand it now. With a few words, she described exactly how I feel about my life. From my darkest moments came the greatest gifts—self-realization, the Whispers of Heaven, and the creation of this book. It was all part of a perfect plan.

This morning, I'm using my wings to fly in harmony with nature and my heart is fluttering with Joy because my mind is not in charge anymore, I am. I decide which direction I want to go and how I want to feel today. I have that power.

Suddenly, I thought to myself, *I don't have a fancy car. I'm not dressed to impress. I don't have money in my pocket. In fact, I don't have anything or anyone with me at this present moment, and yet, I'm at ease and complete. I am with God.*

I'm alive.
I'm in love.
I'm at peace.
And I'm free.

With the breeze in my face, I took deep refreshing breaths and wandered along the riverbank. The sun was shining, trees were casting shadows across the street, and red and golden leaves were blowing around, playing and tumbling all along the lane. I was enjoying a spectacular show. Suddenly, as I was climbing up the hill on the river road, I lost the conscious rhythm of my feet and my mind took over. *Why do we think we need so much to be happy? Why are we so afraid of silence and simplicity?* I used to feel alone all the time; it did not matter if I was at home with my family or out with friends. We live in the big world and yet I felt all alone in the midst of this great Universe.

The Whispers came to me then. *Nancy, you feel alone when you are separated or disconnected from the Universe, your higher Self, from Me. As a result, you experienced isolation. When you feel lonely, you have let your happiness depend on someone or on things. True happiness comes from within. Whenever you feel lonely, know that you have lost touch with your true Self. Don't beat yourself up about it, simply use that feeling as a wake-up call. Don't add frustration or sadness to the feeling of loneliness. Go within and rest in awareness. Silence will give you space around the uncomfortable feeling, space for you to be and to see the truth. In that sacred place, you will quickly remember who you really are, divine energy, one with the Universe. You are never alone.*

Self-understanding may not immediately remove whatever it is that you do not want to feel—in this case, loneliness. However, it will give you the freedom and power to change the intensity of the strong feeling. It will give you the wisdom to respond to it in a healthy way, allowing the unpleasant feeling to resolve rather than carry on. When you feel lonely, take a moment to investigate your thinking. You must explore the thought that caused the pain, the sadness, the fear, or the loneliness. You must look within yourself to understand. Every thought comes from either fear or love—understand which thought is threatening your state of mind. Explore the root cause of your feelings and how you response to it, and reclaim your true self. *The act of being present with what is will make a huge difference in the way your day will unfold. It takes time, courage and honesty to look deeply within yourself, and you cannot have peace until you do. You have to embrace the fear in order to understand it. Remember you have no power over what you have not faced and examined. Step through the fear—welcome the power of love and change your story.*

Know that every single person you meet is part of you, everyone is whole and complete just as you are. No one is above or below anyone else; all people are created equal. Divine energy is all around; it's in everyone and everything. It is in nature. You just need to sit quietly to remember and experience it. The idea of loneliness is a disconnection with oneself, God. You have forgotten where you came from—who you really are. Loneliness comes from not seeing the light within you. Souls thrive on silence. Take a moment to connect with your higher self, and the light in you will shine. You cannot feel lonely if you are connected to God. I am in your breath. Ground yourself in your true being, explore your feelings, and reclaim your whole self. Where there is God, loneliness cannot exist. Breathe consciously and observe the idea of loneliness leaving your heart. Watch your inner self fill up with love and happiness—joy.

When my mind is focused on my breath, I don't try to change anything or anyone. I don't need to be right, I don't need to impress, I don't try to be somewhere else, or obsess about achieving something. I am here, loving *what is*, and if I cannot love *what is*, I accept things as they are, and suddenly the Universe is enough. I am enough. I am with God.

> The more grateful I am,
> the more present I become.
> The more conscious I become,
> the happier days I create.

A PRECIOUS MOMENT

God gives us only the present; invoke the light within you now.

April 6, 2007,

My oldest son Tyeson, who is seventeen years old, is going through his first breakup. After a two-year relationship, he and his girlfriend Stefanie decided to call it quits. Tyeson is a very well adjusted teenager. His focus is on his schooling and music, and I'm very proud of him. However, he was very attached to his dream of the future with Stefanie, so this news was heartbreaking. I could feel his pain as I held him in my arms and tried to comfort him. He opened up to me like never before. I was impressed by his attitude. I knew he was hurting badly and yet he found a way to express his sorrow without anger. He did not put his girlfriend down in anyway. He just spoke about the situation and asked for advice. Although my son is young, he was very much in love with Stefanie; however she decided it was time to move on. Months earlier, they had been making plans for the future and Tyeson was still stuck in those thoughts.

"Mom, talk to me. Help me to ease the pain," he said.

I closed my eyes and asked God to guide me. Suddenly, a poem my best friend Sasha sent me a few years back came to me.

A journey to self-acceptance – A message of hope, love and courage.

> Dear God,
> I surrender this session to You.
> I ask that my interaction with this person (my son) be used for Your purposes.
> I surrender all worldly thoughts I would bring from my past and ask, in this moment, to be filled with Your wisdom.
> May I be used as a channel for Your healing power, for by myself I can heal no one. Rather I remember that Your power within me does the work.
> Show me how to love this person and listen to him and counsel him as You would have me do.
> May I remind him of his own magnificence that through this memory he might awaken to truth.
> May I minister to him truly through Your words and Your thoughts and Your love.
> Amen.
>
> —Marianne Williamson
> *Illuminata*

Inspired by the Whispers, I said, "Tyeson, we all have choices in life about the things we do, say, how we react, and perceive things. We are each 100 percent responsible for our own lives. It may not feel like it sometimes, but our happiness depends *only* on us."

I explained that the world is and will be as we perceive it. When we think that someone else is responsible for our happiness or suffering, these thoughts (lies), make us feel hopeless. When we are constantly telling a sad story and feeling sorry for ourselves, it becomes our belief and we keep on suffering under this illusion.

We have the choice to ease the pain or keep on suffering. We can meet our thoughts with understanding and see the truth.

"Tyeson," I asked, "are you making the situation worse by analyzing it too much? Are you making up stories in your mind? Are you assuming or imagining things that are not facts? By investigating your thinking, you will see the *truth*, and then the madness can end, along with the pain."

We cannot change our situation if we are not aware.
"When we become aware, we take a much-needed rest from the personal stories of our lives; we learn to rest in the present moment. Reality has its place—it hurts to be dumped, but you don't have to make it worse or harder than it really is. Allow yourself to heal; take a break from your sad story. The more you repeat it, the more energy and power you will give it, and the more you will suffer. If you let go, you become detached, and the suffering will fade away."

We create our own story. We are the storyteller of our journey.
I continued, "Life is not always easy, but it can certainly be good. A great attitude is essential for happiness. How we choose to react and think will determine what comes next. Life unfolds moment by moment and what happens at this moment will influence what happens in the next one."

We are all searching for happiness, for what we truly want is to experience *joy*. Joy comes from within. When we live in joy, we live *in love;* we are grateful. Joy is a state of being. It is not a state of doing or having. In a state of joy, we appreciate the good things in life, yet we are aware they could disappear at any time. Joy does not depend on things or people. Joy means living in Spirit, in peace, and in love, therefore, with God. No one is here to make us happy, not even our loved ones. We are the only one with that power.

"It's time for you to create a new story Tyeson!" I told him.

"Take time to breathe mindfully for a while; now center your attention on things that make you feel good—playing guitar, creating music, and being with friends. Be grateful for what you have; a new chapter is beginning. Change is good, and challenges are not letdowns, they are part of life. A challenge is a sign of willingness of the soul to evolve, to understand something new, and to move on to new things. If you let the experience happen without resistance, it will turn into a wonderful thing. This moment is preparing you for something greater in your life.

"On the way through life, we collect tools, tools of awareness, understanding, wisdom, and insight. The more tools we have, the more compassion we will have for others as well as for ourselves. We sometimes need challenges in order to grow; they help to make us better than we used to be. I know you are hurting right now. Nonetheless, it will get better, it truly will, if you give it some time.

"Always travel through life with an open heart, Tyeson. Your heart knows who you are, because your heart is the *real* you, and God lives in your heart. Trust in God's work. *He* knows what *He* is doing. *He* has allowed this to happen to permit you to grow spiritually. You may not feel it now, but this is a perfect moment. You are perfect."

"I love you, Tyeson."

After telling my son all this, I wrote in my journal a few words to Stefanie, also inspired by the Whispers that guided me into sharing my thoughts.

To my dearest Stefanie,

Thank you for giving me a taste of what it is to have a daughter. I miss you very much. I'm so grateful for every hug and the time that we spent together as a family. You brightened my days in so many ways. I wish you well and happiness.

I love you, Stefanie

> When the dog bites, when the bee stings, when I'm feeling sad, I simply remember my favorite things and then I don't feel so bad ...
>
> —Oscar Hammerstein
> "My Favorite Things"
> *The Sound of Music*

COMING BACK TO LOVE

There is a huge difference between fear and caution. Caution moves us forward with care, fear stands still, paralyzed. Avoid paralysis at all cost. It is not good for the soul— and it gets you nowhere.

—Neale Donald Walsch

September 4, 2007,

For the past few days, I've noticed that I'm getting irritated easily, I have difficulty accepting my children's attitude and lack of motivation. I get angry when things are not going my way, particularly when I have to ask my teenage boys repeatedly for the same things. I assume they are old enough now to know better. I expect my children to have a greater level of maturity, dependability, and commitment towards their education and their chores around the house. However, I began to realize my expectations are causing me grief. During the confrontation, I accused my children of being irresponsible and when the screaming was over, I felt awful, as I knew that my behavior was inappropriate.

I sat to contemplate the situation. *You should have known better,* I thought, *and not the other way around. It's your expectations that are creating this misery. For the last couple of days, you have been feeling edgy. You wait for your children to obey your every demand in order to ease* whatever is going on inside you. *Your attitude is far from being pleasant and from this behavior, you expect good results.* Yelling and overreacting never fixes anything. It only creates more inner and outer tension. It wouldn't matter how much you yelled, your children wouldn't never move fast enough for you. What you truly need right now is to go for a walk and meet your thoughts with understanding. The housework can wait until you feel better.

I was not ready at this time to listen to the Whispers. I just apologized to my children and hoped never to act that way again. Expressing my regrets released some of my guilt, however, during the "I'm sorry" speech, I still defended my behavior and therefore, the blame was still with my children and I still felt awful. The next morning, I woke up and saw the light. I did not investigate my thinking sooner because I wanted to be right a little longer. That was the root of my stubbornness.

A few days earlier, I'd had a major fight with my seventeen-year-old son about his future and the unpleasant feeling was still sitting in my heart. Afterwards, he went to school and I stayed home grieving. When my husband arrived from work, I told him how distressed I was. Luke decided to have a talk with Tyeson. They spoke about money, finding a job, transportation, and a place for him to live during his years at university. We, of course, wanted Tyeson to stay home, but Tyeson didn't want to. He wanted to move out and that was that! Even though he did not have any money or a job, he had made up his mind. I became so upset it quickly turned into another argument. We could not agree on anything. I was unaware of the tension building up inside me until, as my voice got louder and louder, I lost it again.

During the argument, I noticed a strange thing happening to me. It was as if I witnessed my behavior as a play or through a monitor screen. I was observing my anger as an outsider and I did not like what I saw. This stopped me from talking anymore and I let my husband continue the conversation, but Tyeson had had enough and rushed to his bedroom. This time, I did not go after him to apologize. I sat, analyzing every part of the conversation. I just wanted Tyeson to consider my suggestion, but he did not want to hear it, and that angered me. I noticed the blame I usually meted out after an argument was not there. My son's "stubbornness" was not the cause of my outbursts. I could see now that my anger belonged to me. I was afraid and worried for my son's future, and therefore I wanted to control his life. I wanted to decide everything for him. I did not want my son to move away because I needed him home so I could control and protect him.

For a moment I struggled with my awareness. I did not want to see this, but it was *all* about me. I was scared. My mind had moved from the present moment into the future, where it was anxious and panicky. I was anticipating, seeing pain—and a lot of it—such as debt, accidents, abandonment, death, suffering, and more suffering. I was caught in the intense FEAR of losing my son. Once again, I had lost faith.

Even though I understood my behavior that night, I left things as they were and went to bed. Tyeson came into our bedroom with a bad attitude and asked what we wanted from him. He was still angry and his attitude provoked me. I was not ready to let go of my intense feelings of fear. I told him to calm down, but I was about to lose it myself. The fear of losing my son was stubbornly sitting in my stomach. I wanted to scream and cry with terror. "You are not going anywhere," I finally said, using the excuse that we didn't have the money to help him to control the situation. My husband kept quiet, but I could not stop yelling. Suddenly, I found myself witnessing my panic again. I was back in the spectator's seat, watching my crazy behavior. I stopped myself and asked my son to go to bed. "Let's talk about this tomorrow when we are both calmer."

Tyeson went to bed angry. I went to bed confused, and my husband turned his back on me. I couldn't sleep. I hated myself. I stayed in bed and thought about my behaviour. FEAR was screaming inside me. I began to cry.

I'm too attached to my children, I'm a control freak. What is wrong with me? Where is my faith? What about God's perfect plan? This letting go of my children seemed to be beyond my capability. I don't know how to free myself from it. Why can't I let them go? Can it be possible? I wondered. My husband turned around and put his arms around me. "Don't worry so much, my love," he whispered gently in my ear. I did not apologize to my son that night. I stayed in bed and suffered. However, something was happening. This was good; I was beginning to see the truth. I closed my eyes, put my hands on my stomach, and began whispering, "I'm sorry Nancy, please forgive me. I love you, I love you, I love you …" I kept repeating the mantra until I fell asleep. I faced the next morning with a better attitude. I knew exactly what needed to be done. I went to my son's bedroom and asked if he would listen to my apology.

"Tyeson, my behavior yesterday was unacceptable and I'm truly sorry. I'm about to make a huge change in my personality. Last night, I recognized the darkness of my behavior. I dislike the angry, screaming person I become when things don't go my way or when fear takes over. This behavior has to stop.

"I need help, Tyeson. Will you help me?" I asked him.

Suddenly his eyes lit up. "Yes, Mom, but what can I do?"

"If I ever lose my temper again, and I'm sorry if I do, ask me to breathe deeply. Just say these six little words, *Mom, please breathe through your nose.* I will know right away that I have lost consciousness. I have lost my way, and fear has taken over. It will bring me back into my body, into the present moment. The power of *love* will find its way back to me. I will then be able to acknowledge my fear and respond in a healthier way, trusting in God's perfect plan again. This will help, I know it will, because *love* will guide me instead of fear. The power of love has healed my broken heart, and I know it can heal my worst fear, the fear of losing you. I love you so much, and I'm sorry for the hurt I have caused you by overreacting. Please forgive me. I am on a journey of growing and evolving. I am willing to change. I am willing to let you go. I am willing to trust in life completely. Just be patient with me, Tyeson. I'm working on liberating myself from my fears. I am replacing them with love."

I could feel the energy changing around me, and the change of energy led my son to apologize, not that he needed to. Moreover, he agreed to consider our suggestions regarding his future, not that he had to. The transformation had already begun. We hugged each other, Tyeson left for school, and I sat in my favorite chair to meditate. I started to cry, and I cried and cried. I said to myself, *I thought I had learned that lesson, and I lost it again.* I reached for my journal and wrote down what I was feeling:

I did not apologize to my son last night, and it's not like me to leave things hanging. How could I stay in bed knowing that my son was in so much pain?

The Whispers answered me: *This time, you have not got yourself out of the situation by asking for forgiveness. You did not make it better for yourself by using the "I am sorry" story. You needed to see and feel. You needed to know where these emotional hurts and fears came from. No more excuses, no more blaming, no more escaping, and no more apologies to flee from the situation. You had to feel the pain, see the pain, and understand the pain.*

Wow, I thought I had dealt with all that pain.

But the word FEAR screamed out once again.

Nancy, you live your life in fear, and it affects the way you think, feel, act, and react. Your behavior is based on fear.

"But why am I only reacting this way with my family, the people I love the most in this world?"

You said it—because you love them so much. You can love your children without being attached—have faith.

"That doesn't make sense; I hurt my family because I love them so much?

Why am I so angry?"

Your fear makes you angry. The fear of losing another child. The fear of your children losing their way. The fear of your family suffering the way you suffered. The fear that someone will not love your children. The fear that someone will judge you or one of your children. The fear of sickness and pain. You have so many fears. Nancy, you are blinded by fear. You respond and act out of fear. The attached love you have for your children makes you believe that you have to protect them always and forever. You do not trust in the moment. You use the name of love to hide your fear and defend your behaviour. Overreacting is a response to fear. The lies you are telling yourself about your children are the reason for your suffering. In order to transcend it, you have to understand it; meeting your thoughts with understanding is the doorway to understand why you act in this way. Only love is powerful enough to overcome darkness. Know that where there is fear, there is lack of love, and as soon as you fill your mind with love, fear can no longer exist. Let go and let the power of love write your story. You can love your children without being attached. Remember who you are and when you feel the fear speaking, replace it with love, think of God. I am in your heart; in your every breath I will be.

Wow. I'm still caught in the past without being aware of it. I'm still living my life in fear, making me overreact. I realize my expectations for my children are too high. I comment on their hair, the way they stand, the way they dress, the way they present themselves to the world. I'm too involved in their lives. I want my children to be presentable at all times, but I need to let go. I need to live my life and let them live theirs.

Wow! My past is still controlling my life; it's in my every thought, decision, and action. I now know anger is masking my fears. Once

I confront my fears openly, I will be able to replace them with love. By embracing the one true force—LOVE—I stop fighting, and the control freak will no longer exist, and my children will be free of my irritability. I will then be able to love them in a healthy way.

As I looked deeper within, I see myself at ten years old, sitting alone in the classroom at my old elementary school. I was shy and afraid, and feeling like an outsider, the one who came from Centre Térèse-Martin, I was called the dirty girl, the ugly girl, the stupid girl. I was either ignored or tormented. My hair was a mess, my clothes were old-fashioned, and I wore them several days at a time. No one wanted to know me. In any teamwork, I was always the last one to be picked. This was humiliating. Partner-work was even more embarrassing; no one wanted to pair up with the girl from the convent. The teacher had to randomly pick someone to be with me. Every day, I heard the whispers of other children saying how filthy and hideous I looked.

Now Jessy's death comes to mind. Losing Jessy created the fear of losing another child, causing me to be overprotective. Nothing bad has ever happened. Tyeson and Spencer are healthy teenagers; besides, their lives are not in my hands. I don't have that power. My role as a parent is to love, guide, and accept them just the way they are, not to control them. Okay, so, I want my children to be successful. I want them to look presentable. Wow! This is truly all about me! I want my children to have what I didn't have. I want them to be loved, respected, secure, and acceptable. I want them to look and behave well so I can feel good, so I can feel safe. God, I have to let go! My children are not me. They have their own paths to follow, and they have their own lives to live. They don't need my baggage, my personal story. I don't want my children to carry my stuff with them all their lives; it's way too heavy. My fears cannot and will not control my children or my life anymore. *Love* is who I am. I want *love* to inspire and direct my every move.

What if I slip back into my old habits? I'm prone to do that, I thought.

The Whispers answered, *Nancy, you are human; you are growing, learning, and remembering. You might slip back from time to time and that's okay. Recognize the fear and remember you cannot have God and have fear at the same time. Stop yourself in a moment of fear and replace it with love. Peace lies in your heart, and the key is love.*

"What can I do when I catch myself overreacting again?"

Notice the real thought behind the feeling; explore the root that is causing the behavior. Investigate and then use the power of love as your mantra. Awareness is the key to self-realization. Find your breath in the background of your story, breathe a few breaths with complete awareness, and you'll find love is waiting for you. If you lose your sense of Self for a moment, apologize immediately to the person you have offended and keep on Loving. You will see how transforming it is to rest in absolute love.

Every experience is an opportunity for spiritual growth. This opportunity was given to you to help you grow. You are growing even at this very moment.

Every thing happens *for* me, not *to* me.

—Byron Katie

FLY AWAY!

Allow yourself to soar to new heights.

February 11, 2008,

I sat in my favorite chair and asked myself, Why *am I feeling so edgy this morning? Should I sit and explore this sadness?*

No, you shouldn't. You need to get on with your day, my mind said.

My soul said, *What you need right now is to listen and pay attention, be with what is. You need to investigate the thoughts that make you feel sad, because when you do that, you will see clearly—you will discover the truth, and then, your whole world will change.*

The Whispers added: **You know, Nancy, the world is as you perceive it. Nothing is truly sad except in your thinking. Meet your thoughts with a loving heart; you have the choice this morning to change how you feel.**

"Okay, okay, I will pay attention. I will sit with *what is*," I said out loud.

From where I was sitting, I could see a portrait of my children on a Chinese cabinet. My eyes rested on Tyeson and my heart sank. "Tyeson, I miss you so very much." And yet my son was right here with me. He had decided to stay home during his years of university, so why was I feeling so sad?

The Whispers: **Go deeper, Nancy. Investigate your thoughts and welcome the pain, see what is behind this sadness.**

Oh God, I know exactly what is bothering me this morning. Today is Tyeson's birthday. He is turning eighteen. He's free to do whatever he wants to.

For years, I told my son, "The day you turn eighteen you will be free to do whatever you want; until then, you have to follow the house rules."

Instead of celebrating my son's birthday, I'm crying about the sudden detachment, about him becoming independent. I am still painfully attached to my son. I just don't know how to let go. *When am I ever going to be able to let go?* I wondered.

It seems I don't really want my son to grow up. I'm stuck in the identity of being Tyeson's mother and nothing else. Who am I, if I'm not his mother? I feel that I'm losing a part of myself. I'm afraid that my son will no longer need me. I feel a big void in my heart.

The Whispers said, *Watch your thinking, Nancy! You are creating this misery for yourself. You are not losing Tyeson or yourself—these thoughts are all lies.*

But if I am not Tyeson's mother, who am I?

Wow! My identity is truly being challenged.

The Whispers continued: *Nancy, a new chapter is taking place in your story. You are simply going through a normal life change. Surrender to it and understand that the sadness you are feeling is coming from the thought of losing Tyeson, but you are not. The role that you have been playing for eighteen years is simply transforming to a new one. You are creating a new story with your son, a new relationship. You will always be Tyeson's mother. Love your son without being attached; attachment generates pain because you are putting the source of your happiness and fulfillment on him. Understand that Tyeson is not leaving you. You will always have a special bond with your son. Your love will connect you forever.*

Consciously or not, Tyeson is going through this transition with you. Together you are going through a beautiful transformation. This is the reality of the situation. There is nothing to be sad about. You should be celebrating! Your son is turning into a handsome butterfly. He is learning to fly on his own, but he is never flying too far away.

Fly free little butterfly, fly free…

—Love mom

THE ART OF MODERATION

> *Moderation is a conscious choice in situations where we have alternatives, and we choose it so that we can maintain balance in our lives.*
>
> —Jean Smith
> *Now!*

Four years ago, three of my good friends and I made an agreement to meet on our birthdays, and last night was one of those occasions. As usual, we talked about everything, and I mean everything. We laughed so much that our stomachs hurt. One of our topics was men. Two of my girl friends are single, out there in the world looking for "Mr. Right." We gossiped about old flames and talked about good and bad experiences. Some of us had seen Dr. Oz talking about healthy poops on Oprah, and in the restaurant, with food in front of us, we discussed the digestive system. We have to be truly good friends to talk about these kinds of intimate details. I love my crazy old friends.

However, when I left the restaurant, I felt uneasy in my heart. I knew what it was, but I did not want to go there. I went home and ignored the feeling all together. When I awoke the next morning, I realized it was still bothering me. I tried to clear my head, but the uneasy feeling was still lingering with me. The feeling was too strong to be ignored, and so I sat silently and waited for the Whispers to come. The word *greed* appeared on the screen of my mind, and I felt regretful, as if I needed to say sorry to somebody.

Before the dinner meeting with my friends, I had made a pact with myself and I intended to stay true to it. I wanted to lose a little weight around my waistline, so I decided to eat a light and healthy meal. Going out to eat is always a celebration. I'm with friends and I don't have to cook. I love fresh hot bread with butter and chocolaty desserts. However, through experience, I know they make me feel bloated, heavy, crampy, and very uncomfortable, and they definitely don't help my waistline. I also know that at times I can be greedy. When this happens, bread and chocolate become like an obsession, I can't stop wanting more. While we were waiting for our food, the basket of fresh hot bread was tempting me. I eyed the bread like a starving hyena and felt its shape, smell, and texture melting in my mouth, and I wanted it. No, I had to have it. Where was my self-control? I made up excuses. I convinced myself that tomorrow I would do better and that I deserved a piece of bread. I was lying through my teeth. Even though I knew that if I had one piece, I wouldn't be able to stop myself, I reached for the basket and grabbed a slice, and just like that, I chose to ignore my gut feelings. Defeated, I took another piece, then another, and then another, when it was time for dessert, I took a bite of the birthday cake, and that was it, I dug my fork in and shovelled the mud chocolate pie into my mouth like Miss Piggy. I was ashamed, but no one knew; I played it cool! Then I decided to think over the entire night and realized that my greed did not stop with the bread or the cake. When dinner arrived, my eyes scanned each plate, not out of curiosity, but greed. I wanted something from everyone's plate. I wanted the mushrooms off France's plate. I wanted the mashed potatoes off Carole's plate. I wanted the red peppers and onions off Suzie's plate. Wow! I didn't appreciate what I had in my own plate; my plate was not enough. I was greedy. I had forgotten how to be grateful for what I have.

Caught between greed and the Whispers, I still chose overindulgence; therefore, an internal war broke out. My pain was voluntarily inflicted. I had chosen suffering over peace, self-control, and moderation, and I knew what was coming next—the regrets, the frustration, and the pain. I had made the wrong decision. There is a lesson in this. When I let my mind take over, I never feel good afterwards. Oops, sorry, I meant I may feel good for a short while, but it never lasts. Following the greedy incident, it did not take long before I felt disappointed. The joy of being with my friends was replaced by bloating, cramping, and irritation, and I was hurting.

I took the dictionary and looked up the word greed. The opposite of greed came up, *moderation*, and then, I started to think about stability, equilibrium, and balance. When I first started yoga, my teacher said to me," You need to work on your balance. Ground your feet, Nancy. Meditate on your first chakra."

That day I read about the chakras. I learned that we have hundreds of energy centers in the body. There are, however, only seven principal ones. The seven major chakras are found from the base of the spine to the top of the head, and together, they form a profound formula for wholeness that integrates the mind, body, and spirit. Each of these chakras is associated with a particular quality. The first chakra is the root chakra, the heart of stability. It's located at the base of the spine. The first chakra is related to survival, grounding, balance, stability, and courage. This energy center is also associated with insecurity, out of balance, anger, *greed*, and self-centeredness. A strong root chakra connects us to earth, giving us stability, strength, and power. The will to live and the feeling of trust and security are at the center of the first chakra. When energy flows freely though the root chakra, we are secure and have balance in our lives. We feel protected and have a strong foundation. My teacher instinctively sensed that I was out of balance.

"Find your feet," she said. "Put them down and discover stability.

"The ground will support you and invite you to let go. Trust. Be here in Tadasana (mountain pose). Bring your mind to your breath. Balance is never too far away. It's in your awareness."

Wow! I now realize that the person I needed to apologize to for my moment of greed was myself.

A moment of struggle can be a moment of great learning. All struggles can be teachers to further our personal growth. We can learn to get out of our own way by sinking a little deeper into awareness, into the present moment. Today I'm working on moderation. I don't have to eliminate the food I enjoy in my life. I just have to find *balance*. Where there is understanding, there is freedom. This story can be used as a metaphor in many situations of our lives.

THE POWER OF FRIENDSHIP

Self-acceptance is realizing that everyone and everything is in me.

— My best friend Sasha

Since I have been committed to writing this book, one particular person has been taking this journey with me, my best friend Sasha. For years now, we have exchanged words of love, understanding, and compassion. We are fortunate to have found someone to grow with, to cry with, to talk over ideas, and also to laugh with. We enjoy sharing and talking about everyday life. Our time together is not about gossiping; we exchange deep and profound thoughts, and for the first time in my life, I have a friendship based on spiritual growth. She is my partner, my spiritual companion. My relationship with Sasha has opened a new door to the meaning of friendship. We have both reached a point in our lives where we want to be happy and peaceful. We want to simplify our lives and support each other with our dreams and goals. We mutually decided to center our conversations on personal growth and happiness. It's not as if we don't talk about anything else, but our conversations always move in the direction of love and inspiration. I'm grateful for my friend; she has been with me through many happy and difficult times. Sasha's deep compassion and understanding has truly helped me over the past twenty years, and without knowing it, we were helping each other.

The weekly conversations we have keep us grounded. It's as if we are renewing ourselves by remembering who we are together. Sasha is very much involved with the writing of this book, maybe not directly, but in my heart and soul. Her words of wisdom are scattered throughout all these pages. She is my fellow spiritual traveler, my best friend, my friend for life. There is something very powerful between two women who share respect and love. The strong bond between us facilitates security and a trust that can never be broken. The strong tie we have helps us during tough times, as well as allowing us to feel joyful for one another during the good times. Sharing life with someone who can relate, understand, and support you is truly magical. In a true friendship, there is no competition or judgment, there is only love and understanding. I'm fortunate to have found a true friend.

During the lowest point of my life, Sasha gave birth to a ten-pound beautiful baby girl, Maya. She had a husband who adored her, and a two-year-old son, Denver. Life was good. She felt truly blessed. In my life, I also had a marvellous husband and two amazing children, and yet we lived in two different worlds. My best friend was happy and I was suffering. There were times Sasha knew little of my state of mind. Although we talked on the phone several times a week, I was not being honest with her. I lied and pretended that life was fine. I believed that my pain would pass and shortly I would be my old self again. Sasha must have been hurt that I didn't have the courage to share my pain with her—after all, she is my dearest friend. That day when she called me at my mother's house, I was surprised to hear her voice and didn't know what to say, but Sasha put me at ease. She simply said how much she loved me and that she would be waiting for me to return. When I went home, I was still suffering. I didn't want to see anyone, so I didn't call Sasha. I stayed in my bedroom, hiding. Two weeks following my return home, Luke said, "Please talk to her. She wants to speak with you." I took the phone and listened to what

Sasha had to say. She asked me if she could come to my house and lay down beside me.

"We don't need to talk, Nancy, I just want to be there for you. Please let me do this. I want you to know I love you and that I'm here for you." It was hard to say no. It had been months since I'd seen her. She lay down beside me and we never spoke. We looked at the ceiling in silence. Tears rolled down my face, Sasha felt my distress and grabbed my hand. Knowing that she was there made me feel safe; it eased my loneliness. She suddenly whispered, "I love you, Nancy. I really do." I felt her love in my heart. Her silence allowed me to feel her compassion; not once did we talk about my condition, and it was nice.

Silence truly speaks, louder than we think. It speaks at a higher level of consciousness; it speaks from the heart. The heart doesn't need words to know, feel, or understand, and it is so wonderful to go beyond words and feel the power of love.

When we truly surrender, we give up trying to change the situation. We give up our opinions, and we don't look for answers. We stop asking, "Why is this happening?" We stopped doing. We are comfortable with silence. When we stop arguing with *what is*, the anxious feelings are replaced by peace. That is what Sasha gave me on that day. Through her silence and stillness, she reduced my anxiety. The touch of her hand felt uncomfortable at first, however when I surrendered to the moment, it became spiritual. I was removed from thinking to feeling, causing the mental noise to calm down. That is the true power of *Being* Present.

I have many angels in my life and Sasha is one of them.
I love you, Sasha. We are friends forever.

A journey to self-acceptance – A message of hope, love and courage.

Friendship

Our hearts entwine forever,
Like a poem or a song.
As I listen to our melody,
We grow forever strong.

In peace and harmony,
We reach each mountain peak.
Sharing joy and sorrows,
A river grew from a creek.

Mingling together with the sea,
We now reach a star.
You are the work of God,
I'll be with you, near or far.

– This poem is for you Sasha
Love Nancy

WHISPERING, "I LOVE YOU."

Open your heart and see the best in yourself and other people.

A friend of mine had met someone through a dating service and had fallen in love. However, later on in the relationship she began complaining about him and seemed unhappy. After two years of living together, her boyfriend left without a word, taking all of his stuff with him when she was away in Québec City. Adding to her pain, he left with a large amount of money that he had borrowed from her. Caroline was devastated. Even though I thought it was a blessing they had broken up, I was sad to see her in so much pain and so I invited her to stay with me for a few days. Caroline couldn't eat, sleep, or even take a shower. I tried my best to support and comfort her. I listened to her hysterical rage, but I did not encourage her bitterness. It was tough to keep quiet, because I wanted to shake her and say, "This is a good thing. You were not happy anyway." But I didn't. That's not what she needed or wanted from me. Those three days were difficult for me, as I was no longer used to so much drama.

Caroline then asked me if I could contact her ex-boyfriend and try to get her money back. After several phone calls, he agreed to meet with me. I learned it was never his intention to keep the money. This was a huge relief for Caroline; nonetheless, she was heartbroken and full of resentment and anger. This lasted for months and she suffered terribly. Then one day, she announced that she was seeing him again.

I was shocked. I could not believe that after all she went through; she had let him into her life again. I was upset. I said to myself, *That's it. I will not help her anymore.* I didn't see my own resentment. How could she forget about all those difficult times? I certainly did not. I heard the cries, saw the pain, and listened to her sad story over and over again. Because of this, I had created a monster in my mind, and so I didn't want to see him or have anything to do with him.

One afternoon, Caroline and I decided to go downtown shopping. On the way there, she said she was stopping at her boyfriend's apartment. I was furious. She didn't ask if I was okay with it or how I felt about it. She knew I was not happy about their reconciliation, and it put me in an uncomfortable position. Caroline had made the choice to have Ray back in her life; however, I hadn't yet made that choice.

I stood behind Caroline as Ray joyfully embraced her, and then he turned toward me, and said, "No hug?" I was shocked. He stepped forward and hugged me. I stood rigid and offended. Caroline and Ray talked for a few minutes. I thought we were leaving, but instead, Caroline entered the apartment and asked Ray to show me the hundreds of pictures he had taken of her that week. I was boiling inside. I was angry with my friend for putting me in such a situation. I said to myself, *When we go, I will tell you exactly how I feel.* Then something amazing happened. I became aware of my negative behavior. It shocked me to see how I was reacting. I asked myself, *Why are you so angry? Why do you have so much hatred toward this man? You are in a very bad place right now, anxious and frustrated. Remember that bad vibes toward someone means bad vibes toward yourself. This is why you feel so bad. Stop for a minute and face the darkness that stands in front of you. Remember that you have no power over what you have not explored. Meet your thoughts with understanding, and then look for the positives, focus on the good vibe with appreciation, and feel the power of love in action.* Within seconds, I started whispering, "I love you. I love you …" I looked into his eyes and imagined him receiving it. I was willing to change my reality. All of a sudden, a smile stole across my face and I felt liberated. I was free of my resentment.

The act of whispering "I love you" had shifted me into a good place; suddenly, I was involved in the conversation and became interested in my friend's pictures. When it was time to go, I hugged Ray good-bye, and not because I had too, but because I wanted to. I wondered if Ray felt the change of energy between us. I sure felt it. On our way downtown, I told Caroline what had taken place. I also said if she wanted a relationship with Ray I would support her, and I meant it. I cannot tell my friend or anyone else what they should do. This is her life, her story. I can only be a friend and support her on the way.

A few days later during a spiritual walk with nature, I thought of Ray, it was amazing; there were no bad feelings. I was loving *what is*.

We all have dark moments, but it doesn't mean we are bad. It means that we are human. When we ground ourselves in the light, we let go and begin to flow with the power of love. Living in a state of love means the heart stays to its divine knowing. When we attack someone, we have forgotten who we really are. In the presence of love, darkness dissipates.

This simple but magical sentence *I love you* had transformed a very uncomfortable situation into a peaceful one. My new mindset had evoked a good feeling within and created a good vibe that transformed the experience. I let go of the old belief and created a new one. Nothing about Ray had changed, just my perception of him. An open heart is an open mind—the power of *love* truly transforms.

Suddenly, I was at peace with Ray, Caroline, and myself.

This is the power of *love* in action.

You must not hate, and must love. Because, just as in the case of electricity, the modern theory is that the power leaves the dynamo and completes the circle back to the dynamo, so with hate and love; they must come back to the source. Therefore, do not hate anybody, because that hatred which comes out from you, must, in the long run, come back to you. If you love, that love will come back to you, completing the circle. It is as certain as can be, that every bit of hatred that goes out of the heart of a man comes back to him in full force, nothing can stop it; similarly, every impulse of love comes back to him.

—The Yoga Sutras of Patanjali
Introduction by Swami Vivekananda

IT'S OKAY TO ASK FOR WHAT WE WANT

Take time to feel the love that surrounds you.

There are new things happening in my life. My son Tyeson just turned eighteen, and believe it or not, I'm adjusting beautifully to this new phase in my life. I'm also writing a new program to teach yoga, hoping it will be accepted in two new schools. In addition to that, I'm planning to open my own yoga studio. While all this can be a bit overwhelming, it's not what is bothering me this morning. My heart felt heavy and I decided to investigate; thinking of my husband, I burst into tears. Something didn't feel right. All of a sudden I felt a need to talk to Luke. I rushed to the phone, but knowing how impulsive I can be in a state of panic, I hesitated. I need to calm down, and I need to explore the thought that makes me feel this way. I suddenly realized that I had been trying to escape these feelings for sometime now. I reached for my journal and began to write down my thoughts:

> *I miss my husband. I miss the laughs, the talks, the walks, and the good times we used to have together. I am overwhelmed by regrets. What has happened to us?* I asked myself.

The Whispers spoke: *Why are you trying to convince yourself that everything is fine when you know that something feels wrong? You don't need to control or escape your feelings. You are disappointed and frustrated—be with it. The key is to surrender and to be true to yourself. Don't you want to know why you are feeling this way? Don't you want to feel better? You can feel better. Pushing your feelings away will just make the matter worse. Listen to your inner guidance. Meet your thoughts with understanding, and the truth will set you free. Ask yourself, why am I feeling this way? What do I need that I am not getting? The more you explore your feelings, the more you will be able to communicate your needs.*

The Whispers continued: *Nancy, it's okay to ask for what you want. Remember, the truth will set you free. You can free yourself from this uncomfortable state of mind. You know what to do.*

I took in deep breaths and wrote down what I wanted.

> *I want romance in my life. I want excitement. I want to go out and have fun. I want to share my feelings and dreams. I want friendship. I want to go for a walk late at night, holding my lover's hand. I want to watch romantic movies and feel romantic. I want to laugh. I want to sit in my favorite chair and talk about everything and yet nothing. I want a hug and a kiss that lasts a lifetime. I want to hear the whispers of love. I want it all, and I want it with my husband.*

Wow! This is incredible. I understand now why I feel this way. I need to share my newfound understanding with my husband, and so I called him.

"Hello," he said.

Tears caught in my throat.

"Hello," he repeated. "What's going on?" he said nervously.

With great effort to hide my sadness, I said, "Can you come home from work? I need to speak with you. It's important."

An hour passed, and then I heard the front door open. Luke walked into the dining room and saw me in my pajamas sitting in my favorite chair. "What is going on?" he said.

Now that he had arrived, I felt embarrassed to ask for what I wanted. I started to cry. "This is not working, we are not working, what has happened to us?" I asked him. "We used to be so in love, and so involved with each other. Our life has become an unexciting comfortable routine. Neither of us makes an effort to keep our relationship alive. We are so caught up with our daily routines, we don't make time for us. I am waiting for you to romance me and you are waiting for me to initiate it. We are doing nothing as a couple anymore. I'm too busy writing my book, teaching, and focusing on my personal development that I'm ignoring us. You are so busy with your work and building Tyeson's truck that you have no time for me. I miss you so much."

Luke listened quietly, so I kept going, "I want the kind of love a man and woman can share together. I know you love me, but where are you in this relationship? I want to hear your hopes and dreams. I want to feel you. Do you feel me right now?" I asked him.

His eyes teared up. "I love you so much, and I've missed you so very much," he said tenderly.

Luke had now found a way to share his feelings with me. This was so amazing— just from investigating my feelings, I had discovered what was bothering me and I was able to ask openly for what I wanted. Incredibly, I found out that my husband had been hoping for this discussion. He just didn't know how to approach me with his feelings. He had just let things be, knowing in his heart we would find each other again, and we did. There will be no end to our love story, because we choose to keep it alive.

The Whispers explained, *Nancy, life is what you make of it. How you experience everything is up to you. The feelings in your heart are the ones that will bring you to your higher self. You always hold the answers in your heart. The time you take to observe what is going on within you, the more you will connect with the Whispers of the Universe and the more joy you will have in your life. It's all about being true to yourself.*

Don't do an evaluation, but an observation. You want to hear and listen to what your heart has to say. I have placed divine wisdom and power in your hands. If you know that love is what you are, you will share it and you will experience it in your life.

Before taking action, ask yourself, Will this decision bring me peace? Will it light up my heart? Will it bring me joy?

The heart is pure and spiritual, and it stands for *love*. It represents compassion, harmony, faith, forgiveness, and healing. People with well-developed heart chakras show great tolerance and openness.

I used to think I came to earth to overcome depression, anxiety, and attachment. I did not come here to overcome anything. I came to awaken, to remember and to experience *love* in all its glorious ways. I want to *feel* my life. I don't want to miss any of its wonderful ups and downs. God gave us the gift to love and it is up to us to use it. We can heal ourselves by using the power of love. Every morning, arise and say, *I will live this day and love this day*, and by consciously whispering *I love you*, know you are making the world a better place for all. The ability to love is in our hearts. We have the power to open the door and heal the world; the key is in our hands.

Love is a state of being in harmony with oneself and the world. Living *in love* is living in a state of grace.

From Love
we were made!
We have a heart that feels;
the beat of our heart is the sound of Love.
Hear your heart.
Listen to its beats.
Reach for them, listen deeper—
God is the sound.
Open your heart to Love,
offer that Love.
Listen deeper—joy is in the beat of a heart.

Sit quietly and try this miraculous meditation:

Place your hands on your belly and breathe
consciously for a few minutes.
As you inhale,
Visualize the power of *Love* entering your body through your nose.
As you exhale,
Imagine sharing that *love* with the Universe.
Let the power of *love* touch every soul on this planet.
Inhale *Love* for yourself.
Exhale *Love* for others.

Inhale *compassion* for yourself.
Exhale *compassion* for others.
Do this for a few more minutes.
Use your imagination.

A journey to self-acceptance – A message of hope, love and courage.

Feel and see how healing this is.
Inhale, *love*
Exhale, *love*
Inhale, *gratitude*
Exhale, *forgiveness*
Feel its vibration
Feel its healing power
It's freeing
It's truly liberating.

I WILL LIVE THIS DAY, AND LOVE THIS DAY.

Let your heart sing and the beauty in you be what you do.

The one question that puzzled me the most in the past was, "What is my purpose in life?" I also phrased it, "Do I have a special talent?" I had friends who knew exactly what their unique talent was—with some it was music, with others, it was drawing, singing, nursing, painting … They knew exactly what they loved to do and were good at it. All my life, I couldn't find anything I was good at. I felt left out, as if God had forgotten me. I believed having a special talent had to be something so big that everyone could see it. It was only when I started dancing that I realized I was good at something. During my dancing days, I became aware that my appearance was getting me attention, comments, and praise. This gave me a false sense of purpose. I was flattered and believed this must be it, and so I considered modeling.

When I stopped dancing, I was lost. Without education, I felt trapped and inadequate. *What am I supposed to do with my life now?* I thought. It was a heavy load on my shoulders and it got heavier by day.

I loved being a mother but needed more in my life. The books I read often talked about how we came into the world with a special gift—that there is an intuitive presence living within us. Some say inspirations come directly from Divine Spirit. When we are in alignment with divinity, we stop searching. We know who we are; we listen to our hearts and ignore what others say we should do.

> *Love is within us. It cannot be destroyed, but can only be hidden. The world we knew as children is still buried within our minds.*
> *Our childlike self is the deepest level of our being. It is who we really are and what is real doesn't go away.*
> — Marianne Williamson
> A Return to Love

Spiritual teachers suggest reaching deep within ourselves and seeing how we truly feel, to find out what made us truly happy as children. Think of the imagery games you played between the ages of six and fifteen and this will help you to find your true passion. When we are inspired, we become creative, we are in our dharma, fully present and in harmony with ourselves. When we are in harmony with what is in our heart, it is the greatest happiness.

At first, your special talent may seem very small; nonetheless, if it resonates in your heart, it will tell you, "Please don't dismiss me!" You need to be vigilant, because you may miss it. Playtime is simple. It could be something like playing with colors, dressing up, fixing friends hair, or being with nature ... it could be something so simple we could overlook it. When we are having fun, we have found our passion. Fully present, we surrender, we give up the "should or should not" of the ego, and we no longer have to try so hard. Playtime is a spiritual practice; it is who we really are.

This is exactly what I did. I watched myself playing as a child; then I could see right away what made me happy. At first, around the age of seven, my favorite thing to do was to play "school." I always wanted to be the teacher and wished the game would never end. Now I am a yoga teacher. When I was at the age of nine to twelve, the nuns put together a group of dancers to entertain the parents at Christmas time. Guess what? I was always picked to be in the front line. All my life, I danced around the house just to have fun. It was my way of expressing myself, and it felt good. Now, I teach a Maya/dance/cardio class, which I created. At the age of fifteen, I started a personal journal, which I kept all my life. I also wrote poetry and this has enabled me to write this book. It's truly that simple.

Between yoga and Maya/dance, I feel I have now the yin and yang, (the tranquil and passive, and the dynamic and active) of my world. My soul needs peace and quiet, which I receive from yoga and meditation. My heart needs to rise up in joy, which I receive from dancing. In addition, I have my writing to keep me in touch with my feelings. In their own unique ways, all three passions keep me present and happy.

My life now has a purpose. I realize that I was meant to accomplish greatness in simple things. That is why I need quiet time to return to my source. I now cherish the little things in my life that seem so simple, but mean so much.

The more open my heart is, the closer to God I become. The more open I am to humanity, the more opportunity I have to give back, and the more I give, the more I receive.

When I am open to all, I embrace life,
I embrace who I am,
I embrace God.

A journey to self-acceptance – A message of hope, love and courage.

Express yourself,
embrace who you are,
love what you do,
listen to your inner music,
play your song,
let the entire world hear your melody,
and have fun on the way.

THE POWER OF LETTING GO

When obstacles arise, you change your direction to reach your goal, you do not change your decision to get there.
—Zig Ziglar

In 2006, I opened a personal bank account in secret and have been saving ever since. My goal was to take my husband on a fabulous vacation, as we had never had a honeymoon. A few months before our twentieth anniversary, I took out my bankbook and gave it to my husband. "Happy anniversary, my love," I said. "I'm taking you wherever you would like to go."

Luke was pleasantly surprised, "How did you save so much money?" he said.

"I have my ways," I said with a happy smile on my face.

The next day, Luke said to me, "I know how much you want to have your own yoga studio. I love you for what you've done, but there is a chance here to realize your dream. We can go on a honeymoon later, when your book becomes a bestseller." He giggled. "Right now, let's use this money to build your studio. I'm willing to give up my garage so you can have your dream."

"Let me think about it," I said.

"What is there to think about? You have a chance here to realize your dream. For two years you have thought about me and saved; it's now my turn to think about you," he said.

Fifteen years ago, we had converted the hundred-year-old barn on our property into a garage. Now, we were changing it into a yoga studio. In May 2008, we started clearing out the garage. It was a challenge, as my husband had stuff piled up to the rafters. During his days off, Luke built two garden sheds sided with barn board, one at the bottom of the hill and the other beside the garage—convenient access for his stuff. We hired a friend as our contractor and the real work started. In the evenings, Luke removed the interior walls, trying to locate the source of a foul smell that turned out to be caused by rodents living in the walls. During this work, Luke discovered the building was not even sitting properly on a foundation. One part was cracked and the rest was sitting on dirt. We didn't expect so much work; it was a devastating discovery. We had to raise the building on one side and underpin it without damaging the frame. We had to redo all the walls and insulate them. To top it all off, the money I saved just disappeared in the process. We had to borrow a large sum of money to continue. Luke expected to finish the studio by September, but I had a feeling it would take much longer. I had worked at a holistic center for five years and hesitated to give my notice, as I didn't want to be unemployed. September arrived and we were far from being finished. Luke realized that it had been a mistake to hire a friend; the workers were unprofessional, the walls were not level, windows were not at the right height, and the work on the siding was sloppy. To make matters worse, we were paying them by the hour. A big mistake!

After a long day at work, Luke fixed the workers' mistakes and rushed around shopping to get whatever the guys needed for the following day. We were now five times over our original budget, and once again, we had to borrow money. It was now October and we were left with a concrete floor that was not even level. The contractor had to redo the work, because at some places the floor was one inch out of level. We discovered that it was impossible to fix a poured concrete floor without first breaking it up. This was a terrifying prospect, because we had all ready installed a heating system in the floor a few inches below. The nightmare didn't end here. The contractor and his workers started to skip days, weeks, months, not showing up on the job. Luke would call, and they'd promise to show, but every day we would wait and they wouldn't come back. This was very upsetting. Finally, they came back in mid April, and made several attempts to fix the floor but soon after, the new concrete on top started to crack. Tensions were rising and the contractor began to lose his cool.

One afternoon while they were all working in the studio, desperately attempting to fix the uneven floor, I heard the contractor screaming at Luke. Hearing the contractor yelling at him felt like a stab in my heart. In the past, my reaction would be to jump in, but I didn't this time. Instead, I sat on the pile of drywall sitting on the driveway and began focusing on my breathing. Within minutes, I began whispering, "I love you, I love you," hoping to touch the contractor's heart. I wanted to change not only the energy around me but *in* me, since I had so many negative thoughts about him. I let my husband deal with him. Luke behaved calmly the entire time. Eventually the contractor took his stuff, ordered his workers to pack their tools, and left the site. He shouted on his way out, "I've have enough of this bullshit. I spent hours trying to fix your fucking floor. It cost me time and money, and you're never satisfied. I'm not coming back."

Oh, my God, I thought. *We're left with the mess; we're stuck with no contractor, an unlevel floor, and no more money.* My heart sank. I didn't want Luke to see me cry so I left and went for a walk. Totally frustrated, I wondered, *Why is it so hard to do this, to get this job done?* Friends and family suggested that we stop everything since it was so challenging and expensive. They believed it was a sign. My heart believed otherwise. I knew it would be the right decision to keep going. All the aggravation made me realize just how much I really wanted the studio. I had a vision, a dream, and I believed in it. I should have been depressed; however, although sad, I remained inspired. It was an awful experience, yet it became a moment to reflect, to exercise faith. I decided to surrender the situation to the Universe. I had been tested in every way and realized how much faith and devotion I now have. I did not allow the stress and the unknown to hold me back. I didn't even feel scared or have an anxiety attack. What's more, I recognized the difference between stress and anxiety; although the situation was stressful, I did not feel anxious. It was a revelation, a moment allowing me to see how much I had grown. I was able to deal with it without going out of my mind. I just let life unfold one moment at a time, not fighting, not resisting, not arguing, realizing that nothing could be done at that moment, so arguing and complaining would not have changed anything, it would only have created more misery. We then hired a new contractor to fix the floor, borrowed more money, and finished the job. When the floor was finally level, Luke decided to complete the rest of the work on his own, doing a marvellous job. On September 14, 2009, a year and a half later, my dream came true; I opened the door to the Emerging Butterflies Yoga Studio.

> *"Exploring our dark side is the gateway to understanding why we do what we do, why we sometimes act in ways that are contrary to the desires of our conscious mind, and why we spend countless hours, days, months, or years judging others and holding on to grudges that only brings us headache, heartache, and dis-ease."*
>
> —Debbie Ford
> *The Shadow Effect*

PEOPLE PLEASER

Be yourself; the world loves you and needs you.

All my life I have been a people pleaser, trying to make everyone love me and approve of me. As a child, I always looked for the right thing to say or do. All I knew about myself were my limitations; I felt inadequate. I had little interest in school, which made it hard for me to learn. I had other things on my mind, like the poor quality of my life. I grew up pretending I knew all the answers, manipulating every situation that came my way, trying to hide my fear. I was scared people would discover the truth about me.

In my twenties, I learned very little. I was in the nightclubs dancing, not challenging myself in anyway. In my thirties, the books that interested me were the ones of spirituality and personal growth. At thirty-eight, I decided that I'd had enough of feeling inadequate, so I decided to go back to school. It was a struggle. I had great difficulty learning and remembering new things. I was anxious and began to question what I was doing. The only answer I could think of was that I wanted to prove to everyone and myself that I was worthwhile. I read about geography, but could not retain the information. I tried history but was uninterested. I began to watch the news so I would be more informed. However, it made me uneasy and anxious. I was forcing myself to do something that wasn't me. I only did it to feel smarter; I thought others wanted me that way. It was a façade, and I was miserable, stressed, and depressed. I wanted to know about the world, the ocean, the weather, and the beauty of nature. I didn't want to read about wars or pain. It would bring too much fear and turmoil into my life. To stay true to myself, I had to let go of what did not feel right in my heart. When I went through the stage of questioning my purpose, I was in a deep depression. I felt empty and alone. Year after year, I couldn't find any answers to my questions; it was devastating for me. Yet I managed to survive without answers. I devoted my time to books, to educate myself about my condition and spiritual growth. By doing so, I rediscovered something very powerful—my passion. When I was a little girl, I loved sharing stories and I always loved to write. My dream was to become a psychologist or a teacher. My passion was, and still is today, to help others. This is why I see my past challenges as a gift—without them I would not be who I am today. I found the answer to the most important question of my life. I am here to share my heart, to share my time, and to share my story. Love, health, joy, this is who I am. I don't need to watch the news to teach me about life or how to be happy. I'm happy and peaceful when I am being true to myself, so I let go and followed my heart.

During the time that I was in night school, I realized I had trouble remembering new things, like names or words I had never heard before. Sometimes I wondered if the acute stress and severe panic attacks my brain had endured for months on end had something to do with my short memory. I couldn't recall being this way in my years at college. After living in Ontario for twenty-four years, I still struggle with the English language, and this, at times, makes me feel inferior.

One afternoon, I was in the middle of my garden pulling out weeds; I had my tool pouch with me, and I was wearing my red plastic shoes and my gardening hat. I truly look like a gardener. I have a beautiful garden, full of color, birdhouses, and bird feeders, with

Chinese lanterns and a Buddha sitting in the middle. The different kinds of flowers make my garden look outstanding. That day, a woman walked up my driveway while I was weeding and asked if she could look around. We started walking and admiring each plant one at a time. She smiled with enjoyment. I watched her and could not believe how comfortable she was wandering around. I continued with my work and then she asked, "What is the name of this flower?"

I immediately felt embarrassed. I wanted so badly to know its name. "I don't know," I replied.

She kept looking around and then she asked, "What about this one?" she said.

"Oh, my God," I felt so humiliated. "I don't know," I said again.

She looked at me with a smile and said, "What about this one?"

Will she ever leave? I thought to myself. I felt like a fraud and humiliated with my gardening hat and tools. I took a deep breath and said, "I'm really good with flowers and very creative, but I cannot remember their names. I'm sorry, but I cannot help you."

She laughed. "Don't worry. I don't remember their names either," she said. And then she went on to talk about how difficult the names of flowers are. "Some of them have even more then one name, so it's no wonder we don't remember their names," she said with amusement.

I sat down and contemplated about what just happened. I thought, *My attitude has to change. I have to stop being so hard on myself. I have the right not to know their names. It doesn't mean I'm stupid or inadequate. It simply means I don't know the answers. I must be able to say* no *without feeling bad, without feeling inferior. It's okay not to know the answers. My responsibility is to myself, it's impossible to please everyone. I can say no from a place of love rather than fear.* I choose to feel GOoD. I choose love.

It's empowering to know that I can rise above my thoughts of fear and find peace. The situation may remain the same (having difficulty remembering names), but I can change my response to it. I can change the experience. I can say *no* with a heart that knows I am good enough. I can stop and remind myself I am perfect just the way I am.

I gave myself a gentle pat on the back, and headed back into my garden.

I say *yes* to freedom, *yes* to harmony, *yes* to being real, and *yes* to being me.

I am enough!

A KNOCK FROM HEAVEN

Allow miracles to happen.

May 22, 2010, from my personal journal

Two months ago, in the middle of the afternoon, I heard a knocking sound that seemed to be coming from my front door. I looked outside and there was no one there. A few minutes later, I heard the knocking again. This time it was persistent. I followed the sound and discovered a beautiful female cardinal tapping on the living room window. She had a bright orange-red beak. It seemed very strange that a bird would constantly hit a glass window that hard. *It must hurt,* I thought. I had never seen a bird behaving in such a manner before. Hours later, she was still there knocking. I tried to chase her away by pressing my face against the window. However, she returned the moment I moved away, and this obsessive behavior lasted until seven o'clock in the evening. The next morning, I heard the incessant tapping again. I couldn't believe that she was back. It was 6:30 a.m. and I watched as she flew from the pine tree to hit the glass hard repeatedly. It almost seemed to me as if she was trying to break the window to come inside. Obviously, she could see her reflection and I wondered if this had anything to do with her strange behaviour. By eleven o'clock, I'd had enough. It was becoming quite annoying. I tried everything thing I could think of to scare her away. I tapped on the glass with my fingers and closed the drapes. I also placed a statue of a Buddha's head in front of the glass, hoping this would distract her. There seemed to be nothing that would deter her from her mission. She returned every day, and this became very unnerving. I was being driven to distraction and getting ready to run outside and chase her away. I wanted to scare her off to get a little peace and quiet. Weeks passed and everyday the cardinal was still tapping at the window from 6:30 a.m. until dusk. The constant noise was starting to annoy my sons, as the window was close to their bedrooms. We had to find away to make her stop before she drove us all mad.

A few weeks ago, my friend Sasha had mentioned to me that she had met a psychic at a bookstore. The woman, Kim, gave ten-minute readings with the purchase of her book, and as an introduction, Kim talked about an experience she herself had with a robin flying into her bedroom window. She described this as becoming torturous, and that it continued day after day, waking her at dawn. I sent Kim an e-mail explaining that I also had a bird behaving in the same manner, and wondered if she could give me some advice on how to stop it. She replied, "Call me," and gave me her phone number.

Kim told me her story. "It had gone on for a few years," she said. "The bird came back every spring and left again in the fall. I tried everything to scare the bird away, but nothing worked." She then asked me if I was on a mission and was procrastinating in the process. This seemed to be a strange question, but knowing she was a psychic, I replied that I was trying to finish my book. I'm hoping to publish it.

"I guess I am procrastinating," I said.

"This is why the bird is knocking at your window. It's a wake-up call. The bird is behaving in this way to get you moving," she said.

She told me she had also procrastinated when writing her book and the robin had knocked at her window to remind her to get up and start writing. When her book was published, the bird flew away and never returned.

Later in the day I sat facing the window and waiting for the cardinal to arrive. When she appeared, I asked her what she wanted of me. I also inquired as to whether her brain would be okay after all that banging. It had been nine weeks since I'd heard the first knocking. The cardinal still comes every day, but for a shorter period of time. Some friends of mine came to see her and we tried to take pictures and video her activity. I know now she visits me to get me moving, and I have become very fond of her. I look forward to her wake-up calls; it's obviously a gift from heaven.

On Mother's Day, I decided not to write in the morning. I let Spencer, my younger son, use the computer to play games. However, I said I wanted the computer around three o'clock in the afternoon to spend sometime writing. Lost in a good book, time slipped by. I didn't hear the bird tapping for quite a while. All of sudden, she arrived, tapping at the window. I asked Spencer what time it was. "It's four minutes to three," he said; I had to laugh. The bird had come to wake me up once again. It was time to write. This was truly amazing.

A month later

This morning Sasha called, and while we talked, I was also looking out the window into my garden. There was a spectacular show going on right in front of me. There were six types of birds in my garden: an oriole was sucking juice out of the hummingbird feeder, a blue jay, three yellow finches, two chickadees, and a few sparrows, along with the cardinal that taps on my window. My husband and I have been watching birds for weeks, and one afternoon, Luke gave the birds names. He named the cardinal Sophia.

I've told Sasha I was mesmerized by the beauty of nature. "I've never seen anything like it. I walked outdoors in my youth, but noticed nothing. I didn't see the beauty of the trees, the vivid colors of the flowers, the love and tranquility of nature. The noises in my head were blinding me, obstructing my view. Now, I can see, I see squirrels jumping from limb to limb. I see the green of the trees and hear the birds singing. I notice beauty everywhere. We were lost in our conversation, and I lost track of time. "Oh, God," I yelled. "I'm almost late for work. I'm teaching a Maya/dance class in five minutes." I rushed out to the studio just as my students started arriving.

How perfectly wonderful it is to have your own yoga studio on your property! However, as I walked toward the studio, I noticed a bird in the middle of the driveway. My heart sank. It was a female cardinal. *Sophia*, I thought in panic. I wanted to cry; it looked as if the bird had hit the window of the studio. I was so upset. I couldn't look at her body, I just covered her with a box. It was very hard for me to teach that morning. When the class was over, I called Luke at work and told him the devastating news. "Are you sure she is dead?" he said. "Maybe she's just knocked out."

I walked out and looked at the bird one more time. "Yes, she is dead, but her beak is not as red. Do birds lose the color of their beaks when they die?" I asked.

"I don't know," Luke said. I felt a little hope. I ran back into the house to wait for the tapping. Half and hour passed and still no visitor. I was nervous so I decided to write down my feelings, when suddenly I heard a cardinal in the garden. I rushed outside, but as I opened the door the female cardinal flew away and I didn't see her beak. I went back to the computer and waited again for the tapping. Within minutes, I heard drumming on the window. Sophia was back. It was wonderful, although I still felt sad about the other bird.

I watched Sophia knocking at the window with tears in my eyes. It was strange, it felt as if I had lost a close friend. Sophia has been part of my life for three months; she had become part of our family, like a cherished pet.

At two o'clock, I went for a walk and about a hundred feet away from my driveway, I noticed another female cardinal, dead on the road. She had been hit by a car. I looked at her closely and saw that her beak was bright red. *What is happening?* I thought to myself. Afraid it was Sophia, I rushed back home and waited again for the tapping on the window. I sat in silence asking myself, *What am I doing?* It's okay to love Sophia, but it isn't right to fall apart like this. Sophia is part of my dream, but she is not responsible for my dream. I went deeper into my thoughts and realized that I felt as if anything happened to Sophia it would be a premonition that my book would fail. This, of course, was a foolish superstition and it had to stop. I'm responsible for my life. I make my own dream, my own story. With her or without her, I will do well, I will finish my book and it will be published. When it's time, Sophia will fly away, and I will miss her visits and the beauty of this messenger from heaven, and I will be okay. I trust in that.

Suddenly, I heard a tap on my window again.

God, when a storm hits,
let me see where it can serve me in my life.
Can you hear my thoughts?
Feel my pain.
Read my heart.

May your words reside within me all day long!
Let my actions sing your song,
my eyes see your light,
my feet walk your path.

The time to start is now.
The place is here.

Where there is love,
there is God;
where God is,
there's no fear.

Love is the language of the soul.
Through its power,
we emit divine thoughts and actions.
We travel with compassion, devotion, and trust.
We can rest peacefully,
because we are loved and protected.
We all are.

HOW CAN WE HELP?

> *Ultimately, the healing of the world will emerge not from our changing and correcting others, but from our willingness to change and correct ourselves. Since all minds are joined, our ability to self-correct has a corrective influence on the entire universe.*
> - Marianne Williamson
> *The Shadow Effect*

Wanting to help make the world a better place can be a lot of pressure. I may not be able to take on this responsibility to its fullest, but I can make a difference right now.

My heart speaks:
    From the very first breath we take, divine energy flows through us. God is eternally with us. His essence travels through the veins of humanity and He is the root of all things. Every day He chooses to rejuvenate and renew Himself through nature, the animals, and the souls of human beings. I recognize Him whenever I become aware of the trees around me, the birds flying above, the color of flowers, and the spiritual *heart* of every living thing. My responsibility is to raise my consciousness to love. I want to love as much as possible. The only way I can give love is to fill myself with it. Gratitude is the highest expressions

of love. I say with my heart, I thank you God for this day, for the sun, for the rain, for the plants, for the air we breathe, for the earth, for my life.

Through the words I say and the actions I take, I know I am delivering messages into the world. Each day, I invite God into my thoughts and ask for His guidance. I want to know what He has to say. What can I do to help today?

I want to give back and offer my best to the world. I know I can help through my words and prayers, through my yoga teaching and my daily actions, a friendly hug, a smile, and by simply whispering *I love you* to whoever comes my way. Peace begins within me. I know that I can do this right here and now. We all can. I trust in that.

> Let's enjoy this world. Let's enjoy one another. We are meant to love one another, not to hate one another. Let's stop believing that our difference makes us superior or inferior to one another. Let's not believe that lie. Let's not be afraid that our different colors make us different people. Our legacy is love; it's joy; it's happiness.
>
> —Don Miguel Ruiz & Don Jose Ruiz

To all Emerging Butterflies,

We can live with grace and together we can make a difference. Fly with me, Whisper *I love you* on your way to life. It takes no time at all, and yet it does wonders.

Earth is a place of Grace.
If you do not love everyone,
Try to see them as part of *you*,
One with *you*.

Open your heart, and your mind will open up to love.
Love is the most powerful feeling there is.
It's the Greatest Healer.
It's liberating.
It's who we are.

Sing *I love you* on your way through life.
Feel its vibration.
Watch its power.
We can create miracles.
Truly, we can.

SELF-HEALING MANTRA

I always knew that I was different, I just never knew how wonderful I am.
— *Courageous Butterfly*

With the help of Louise Hay's book *You Can Heal your Life*, I put together positive affirmations that help me through tough times. I use these affirmations as mantras during my walks or before meditation. I find them helpful, keeping me focused and aware.

I am

I am willing to release the old patterns in my consciousness,
to create new ones.

I recognize my unhealthy habits,
and I am creating myself anew.

My mind is a tool.
I use it now in a positive way.
I choose thoughts that make me feel good.

It's wonderful to be me.
I am unique and powerful.

A journey to self-acceptance – A message of hope, love and courage.

I am now creating a safe and happy life,
and I trust in the flow and process of God's work.

I trust my inner voice to reveal to me
whatever it is I need to know.

My inner child is
forever nurtured by me.

I am one with the power that created me, God.
Divine ideas are expressed through my heart.

I let others be themselves,
and I am free.

I choose to live my life in the present moment,
and I am doing all I can.

I am successful,
and there are people who are looking for exactly what I have to offer.

I stand tall and stand in Truth.
I choose to be real, to be me.

I trust that whatever I need to know is revealed to me
at the right time and place.

I am at peace with who I am, and where I am in my life.
One day at a time, I am grateful.

Courageous Butterfly

My true power is within,
and my breath will lead me there.

I am responsible for my own happiness.
I am taking action.
My new world is a reflection of my new thinking.
All is perfect,
I am perfect,
I am complete,
I am.

I honor the courage and the power that lives within me.
I honor the love, the compassion, and the
strength that lives within me.
I honor the creativity, the vision, and the dream that lives in me.

I honor the physical and spiritual person that I am.
I honor and respect the divinity and
individuality that lives within *all* of us.

I value my existence and every living thing on this planet.
I accept, respect, and love others and myself.
I am, just as I am, complete, whole, joyful;
therefore, healthy and content.

I am all that.
I am.
We all are.

A journey to self-acceptance – A message of hope, love and courage.

I learned a wonderful poem from my Tai chi class.

>
> Heavenly Dance
> I am, I am
> I am the One
> I am the All
> I am Heaven and Earth
> I produce yin and yang
> I combine them into one
> Thus, I create everything
> And I destroy everything
> Then I resurrect them again
> And destroy them again
> I am eternal
> I am universal
>
> Yet, I am Nothingness
>
> —Zen Qi Internal Art

AFTERWORD

I just want to let you know …

Even after remembering where I came from, I did not overcome the feelings of nervousness, sadness, anger, and greed, and I did not stop overreacting. These feelings are still with me to this day, the only difference being that I am now aware of them. Therefore, I have the choice to do something about them or not. I have learned to sit quietly with *what is*, and have the option to meet my thoughts with understanding. Investigating my thoughts, I see the truth. I know I can reduce the intensity of my negative emotions by replacing them with love, and then the madness ends. I want you to know that I still make mistakes and still struggle with my ego each day. I have much to remember and understand, because every day is a new day.

After putting aside my book for a few months, I decided to read it again, as if for the first time. I was amazed at how it made me feel. I could not believe its contents came from me and I realized I didn't write this book alone. I recognize a greater power influenced my writing; it came from influential messages that inspired me, and I know God had something to do with it.

At the time of writing this book, I was in a good place, in good hands, and I still am. This book is meant to be shared. I wrote it for my children and for you, my dear readers, hoping I have touched your hearts. During the four years of writing, I realize I also wrote it for myself. It has been therapeutic and awakening. Occasionally, I'm prone to fall back into old habits; now I have something to go back to, to refresh my memory, to keep me on track, to remind me that *love* is all there is, the *one* great force, the highest state of being. It connects us to God and to each other. Together we can help one another to remember, as surely, there is a reason you've been made aware of this book. Collectively, we can make our world a better place, truly we can. *Love* is our hope for a better future. We can rewrite our life stories and create a new dream. We are *all* messengers from heaven, and we can change the kind of messages we send into this world. We can choose to speak the language of love, the language of God, rather than fear and hatred. Bring *love* into your everyday life stories, and see for yourself the changes you create.

My goal is to inspire you to find comfort in God's perfect plan, nothing more and nothing less. It's just that simple.

Hope, Love, Courage, trust the song of your heart. This is my message.
To one courageous butterfly from another, *I love you.*
Nancy Forbes

ROSEMARY'S STORY

Where there is joyous excitement, there is also truth.
I know it's true—because my heart is telling me so.

When I was first introduced to my mother-in-law we had a strained relationship. I felt I was not good enough for her son. We could not agree on most things, and being a "typical" mother, she was very protective of Luke, even though he was a grown man. I could feel her embarrassment and discomfort each time we met. Although we lived only a five minute walk from each other, we had not spoken for years. One day she telephoned Luke and asked him if I would like a grand piano for Spencer, as he was taking piano lessons. Within an hour, a baby grand piano arrived on a forklift at our patio door. This gave us a new opportunity to talk and work on our relationship, and the tension began to ease. We gradually learned to accept each other's differences without arguing. I, however, wanted more. One morning I awoke and made a promise to myself that I would never fight with anyone again, and would let go of my past resentment towards my mother-in-law. I wanted to love her unconditionally, so I began to whisper, "I love you, Rosemary," whenever we met. Rosemary then started to come to my yoga classes, where she is well liked by the other students. At first, I wondered if she came to judge me, as I was still a bit insecure. However, she came to support me, and I soon began to look forward to seeing her in my classes. I had previously asked her to correct my English, to improve my language skills; unfortunately, she did so in class, which made me uncomfortable and I mentioned this to her. She apologized and agreed not to do it again in class. Until we take complete responsibility for our *own* experience, we cannot change it. The moment I felt uneasy, I took action, I investigated my feelings, and then I did something about them. I decided to be honest with her. I was able to express my feelings without anger or being afraid, and what a great result!

Each week Rosemary comes to class and applauds me; this is unusual in a yoga class. Some of the other students giggle and then join in; no one knows she is my mother-in-law. Rosemary doesn't care if she's the only one applauding, she continues to do so.

We are working on my book together. Her writing abilities are amazing. She is a poet and has written almost two thousand poems since April 2009. She is truly outstanding. I have included two of her poems in this book. She writes under the name Rosemary St. John. We are now supporting each other in every way we can. I don't have to whisper *I love you* every time I see her. It is here, in my heart. We truly have become the best of friends. I love you, Rosemary.

I Shall Remember

> The golden eye of day appears
> low in the morning sky
> as softly on the wings of night
> the moon shall say good-bye.
>
> Daylight once more shall welcome
> the day and its new spring,
> while gently as a falling leaf
> birds fly upon the wing.

It's then I shall remember
while I sigh a little sigh,
recalling days so long ago,
too fleetingly flown by.

I feel again your gentle touch
in every summer breeze,
as soft, your spirit lingers,
with love songs of the trees.

—Rosemary St. John
dedicated to my grandson Jessy

To my husband Luke

I knew from the start you were my soul mate and to this day, I believe you are. I have decided to write this letter to show my appreciation for you.

Luke, you loved me unconditionally from the very beginning and I know that you will love me this way until the end, because it is who you are. Throughout the years you have showed me the true power of love, how to love completely, because there is nothing missing in my life. I have respect, friendship, trust, and love. Perhaps I could have a bit more romance—I know you are smiling right now!

In my darkest moments, you were there with me, always strong and willing to help. Not once did you make me feel that you'd had enough and wanted out. Not once did you ever complain; you stood by me no matter what. You have used the power of love to keep me safe and warm. Every single day, you make sure I am okay. You affectionately tap my butt on your way out, just to let me know that you love me. From whispering *I love you* to me and telling me that I look great, to doing thoughtful things around the house, at all times you give your best. You make sure that I am comfortable and at peace—believe me, my love, I know how loving and thoughtful you are.

The work you do with your hands is incredible. You just finished building my yoga studio and you did an amazing job; you did it with love. Everything you do is without condition or judgement; you are perfect and so is my studio. Thank you.

Wow! Twenty-three years already ... It's almost impossible to put into words how I feel about you. I am truly blessed. We talk often about how lucky we are to have found each other. I feel like the luckiest person on earth to have you by my side. We know what we have and we know it's forever. It feels safe and good to share this commitment of love and respect, and to cherish one another so much.

I want the world to know how remarkable you are, as I do. I am in love with the most amazing person on the planet. I can see us, in our sixties, seventies, eighties, walking under the trees, sharing thoughts, holding hands, and pausing for kisses from time to time. I can see us happy, healthy, and content. I know our love is forever. After all these years, I still know you are the one, as you still take my breath away and still give me butterflies in my stomach.

In spite of the tough times we've had, I choose to remember your love and loyalty. I know I would not have survived without your comfort and support. You have helped make my life easier each and every day. Never did you tell me what to do, how to dress, how to look, or what to say, not even once. I've always been free to live my life and be myself. You love me just the way I am. You probably don't know this, but you are at your best always. You are the perfect husband, and I know you are, I feel it in my heart. You make me feel loved and wanted always. There is no jealousy or competition between us, and I love the fact that we constantly bring out the best in each other.

I was hard on you at times, and probably loved you conditionally.

I am sorry. I now know how to love you—I hope that you know how much I do.

I loved you from the very beginning, and I will love you to the end.
Forever and ever,
Your wife, Nancy

To Tyeson and Spencer,

You have a great father; spend time with him, learn from him, enjoy him, and appreciate him because we are so blessed.

I love you,
Mom xoxo

There were people who inquired as to how Luke could deal with my dancing days, and they asked me if he ever demanded that I stop. Allow me to explain the situation. When we first met, I made it very clear to Luke that my past was rooted in my heart and I had made a promise to myself. I swore never again would I let anyone put their hurtful hands on me or tell me what to do, or where to go, or how to dress, or how to live my life in any way. I had learned this lesson the hard way. I now knew what I definitely did not want in a relationship. I also told him I would never cheat on him or be dishonest, because it is not who I am. I am honest and trust worthy, and I expected the same from him. I know that, coming from an exotic dancer, this could have sounded strange, but I did not see myself as a bad person. My heart was always in the right place, and this is what Luke saw, my heart. Therefore, he never asked me to stop dancing or told me how to live my life— although I'm sure he was very happy on the day I quit. He never made me feel bad or uncomfortable about my dancing days. Luke has the best quality a person could have—he lives his life with an open mind and an open heart, and he fell in love with the best part of me, my heart.

One day we were invited to a wedding, and a friend of Luke asked if he could dance with me. As we were dancing together, Kirk laughed and said," This is so amazing!"

"What is so amazing?" I asked.

"You and Luke," he said.

"What about me and Luke?" I asked again.

"Luke knew he was going to marry you long before you guys started dating."

"What do you mean?" I asked.

"One day at the club, Luke said to me, 'You see that girl over there?' pointing at you, 'I am going to marry her.'"

When I returned to our table, I asked Luke to dance with me and whispered in his ear, "So you knew you were going to marry me before you even asked me out."

Luke looked at me with the most beautiful smile and shining eyes.

"Kirk told me." I said.

At that moment, I loved him even more, if that was possible.

"I'm surprised you opened up to him about me. You usually don't open up that easily." I said.

Luke kept smiling. I think he was a bit embarrassed. However, I was glad that Kirk had told me. It makes me feel good to know how Luke felt about me from the very beginning of our love story.

Crazy for your love

You can tell me I'm as crazy
as the silver moon above
who stalks the night in silence,
in search of those in love.

Love is an emotion
so sublime.
It lifts a heart up high
and knows no time.

Crazy for your love
I'll always stay.
True love shall last
until our final day.

As blessed as the songs
the song bird sings
to lift my heart up high,
on angel's wings.

Crazy for your love,
I have no choice.
A melody's the sound
of your soft voice.

No other could I love
if we should part.
In your hands you hold
my trembling heart.

—Rosemary St. John
August 26, 2010

READING REFERENCES

Bassett, Lucinda. *From Panic to Power: Proven techniques to calm your anxieties, conquer your fears, and put you in control of your life.* New York: HarperCollins Publishers, 1995. Print.

Byrne, Rhonda. *The Secret.* New York/Hillsboro, Oregon: Atria Books/Beyond Words, 2006. pg ix-4-9-23-63-81-82. Print.

Bradley, Dinah. *Hyper-Ventilation Syndrome: A Handbook for Bad Breathers.* New Zealand: Tandem Press, 1991. pg 14. Print.

Chopra, Deepak, Debbie Ford, and Marianne Williamson. *The Shadow Effect: Illuminating the Hidden Power of Your True Self.* New York: HarperCollins Publishers, 2010. pg 2-32-96-168.Print.

Dyer, Dr. Wayne. *10 Secrets for Success and Inner Peace.* Carlsbad, CA: Hay House, Inc., 2001. pg 21-139. Print.

Dyer, Dr. Wayne. *There's A Spiritual Solution To Every Problem.* Carlsbad, CA: Hay House, Inc., 2001. pg 148-221. Print.

Dyer Dr. Wayne. *Getting in the Gap: Making Conscious Contact with God Through Meditation.* Carlsbad, CA: Hay House, Inc., 2003. Print.

Dyer, Dr. Wayne. *Wisdom of the Ages: A Modern Master Brings Eternal Truths into* HarperCollins Publishers, 1998. pg198. Print.

Hay, Louise L. *You Can Heal Your Life.* Carlsbad, CA: Hay House, Inc, 1999. pg 60-68-117. Print.

Katie, Byron, and Stephen Mitchell. *Loving What Is: Four questions that can change your life.* New York: Three Rivers Press, 2002. pg 3-4-19-188-227. Print.

Mitchell, Stephen. *Bhagavad Gita: A New Translation.* New York: Three Rivers Press, 2000. pg 58-59-79-91-93-94-95. Print.

Myss, Caroline. *Entering the Castle: Finding The Inner Path To God And Your Soul's Purpose.* New York: Free Press, Simon & Schuster, 2007. pg 50-51. Print.

Ruiz, Don Miguel, and Don Jose Ruiz. *The Fifth Agreement: A Toltec Wisdom Book.* San Rafael, Ca: Amber-Allen Publishing, 2010. pg 39-52-58-63-68-106-107-128-135-142-174-224. Print.

Smith, Jean. *Now! The Art Of Being Truly Present.* Somerville, MA: Wisdom Publications, 2004. pg 106. Print.

The Dalai Lama. *An Open Heart: Practicing compassion in everyday life.* Time Warner Trade, 2001. pg 84. Print.

Tolle, Eckhart. *A New Earth: Awakening to your Life's Purpose.* New York: Penguin Group, 2005. pg 67-158-159. Print.

Tolle, Eckhart. *Eckhart Tolle's Findhorn Retreat; Stillness amidst the world.* Novato.Ca: New World Library, 2006. pg 48. Print.

Tolle, Eckhart. *The Power Of Now: A Guide To Spiritual Enlightenment.* Vancouver, BC: Namaste Publishing Inc, 1997. Print.

Van Praagh, James. *Talking to Heaven: A Mediums' Message Of Life After Death.* New York: Penguin Group, 1997. Print.

Van Praagh, James. *Healing Grief: Reclaiming Life After Any Loss.* New York: Penguin Group, 2000. Print.

Vivekananda, Swami. *The Yoga Sutras of Patanjali.* London: Watkins Publishing, 2007. pg 3. Print.

Walsch, Neale Donald. *Home with God: In A Life That Never Ends: A Wondrous Message Of Love In A Final Conversation with God.* New York: Atria Books, 2006. pg 12-14-15- 81-206-230. Print.

Walsch, Neale Donald. *Conversation with God: an uncommon dialogue: book 1.* New York: G.P. Putnam's Sons Publishers, 1995. Print.

Williamson, Marianne. *A Return to Love. Reflections on the Principles of A Course in Miracles.* London: HarperPerennial, 1993. pg xxiv-154-188-189. Print.

Williamson, Marianne. *Illuminata. Thoughts, Prayer, Rites of Passage.* New York: Random House, 1994. pg 235-236. Print.

Pay it Forward

CPSIA information can be obtained at www.ICGtesting.com
226914LV00002B/109-603/P